T0319113

Cambridge Elements ≡

Elements in Applied Linguistics
edited by
Li Wei
University College London
Zhu Hua
University of Birmingham

VIRAL DISCOURSE

Edited by
Rodney H. Jones
University of Reading

CAMBRIDGE
UNIVERSITY PRESS

University Printing House, Cambridge CB2 8BS, United Kingdom

One Liberty Plaza, 20th Floor, New York, NY 10006, USA

477 Williamstown Road, Port Melbourne, VIC 3207, Australia

314–321, 3rd Floor, Plot 3, Splendor Forum, Jasola District Centre,
New Delhi – 110025, India

79 Anson Road, #06–04/06, Singapore 079906

Cambridge University Press is part of the University of Cambridge.

It furthers the University's mission by disseminating knowledge in the pursuit of
education, learning, and research at the highest international levels of excellence.

www.cambridge.org
Information on this title: www.cambridge.org/9781108986625
DOI: 10.1017/9781108986465

© Rodney H. Jones 2021

This publication is in copyright. Subject to statutory exception
and to the provisions of relevant collective licensing agreements,
no reproduction of any part may take place without the written
permission of Cambridge University Press.

First published 2021

A catalogue record for this publication is available from the British Library.

ISBN 978-1-108-98662-5 Paperback
ISSN 2633-5069 (online)
ISSN 2633-5050 (print)

Cambridge University Press has no responsibility for the persistence or accuracy of
URLs for external or third-party internet websites referred to in this publication
and does not guarantee that any content on such websites is, or will remain,
accurate or appropriate.

Every effort has been made to trace the owners of copyright material included in this
Element. The publishers would be grateful for any omissions brought to their notice
for acknowledgement in future editions of the Element.

Viral Discourse

Elements in Applied Linguistics

DOI: 10.1017/9781108986465
First published online: February 2021

Rodney H. Jones
University of Reading

Author for correspondence: Rodney H. Jones, r.h.jones@reading.ac.uk

Abstract: This Element consists of ten short pieces written by prominent discourse analysts in the midst of the COVID-19 pandemic. Each piece focuses on a different aspect of the pandemic, from the debate over wearing face masks to the metaphors used by politicians and journalists in different countries to talk about the virus. Each of the pieces also makes use of a different approach to analysing discourse (e.g. critical discourse analysis, genre analysis, corpus assisted discourse analysis) and demonstrates how that approach can be applied to a small set of data. The aim of the Element is to show how the range of tools available to discourse analysts can be brought to bear on a pressing, 'real-world' problem, and how discourse analysis can contribute to formulating 'real-world' solutions to the problem.

Keywords: COVID-19, health communication, media, discourse analysis, research methods

© Rodney H. Jones 2021

ISBNs: 9781108986625 (PB), 9781108986465 (OC)
ISSNs: 2633-5069 (online), 2633-5050 (print)

Contents

Contents

Contributors

Elisabetta Adami is Associate Professor of Multimodal Communication at the University of Leeds. Her current research interests are focused on developing a social semiotic multimodal approach for the analysis of trans- inter- and cross-cultural communication. She is editor of Multimodality & Society, coordinates PanMeMic and leads Multimodality@Leeds.

Erhan Aslan is Lecturer in Applied Linguistics at the University of Reading. His current research focuses on digital communication, particularly the analysis of multimodal digital texts such as internet memes.

Carmen Lee is Associate Professor in the Department of English at the Chinese University of Hong Kong. Her research interests include digital discourse and multilingualism.

Christoph A. Hafner is Associate Professor in the Department of English, City University of Hong Kong. His research interests include specialized discourse, digital literacies, and language learning and technology.

Sylvia Jaworska is Associate Professor of Language and Professional Communication at the University of Reading. Her main research interests are in professional discourse in media, business and health settings.

Rodney H. Jones is Professor of Sociolinguistics at the University of Reading. He has published widely in the areas of health communication and mediated discourse analysis.

Wing Yee Jenifer Ho is Assistant Professor at Department of English, City University of Hong Kong. Her research interests are multimodality, translanguaging and learning 'in the wild' using digital technologies. She is also interested in exploring new qualitative research methods for digital research.

Zhu Hua is Chair of Educational Linguistics and Director of MOSAIC Centre for Research in Multilingualism in School of Education, University of Birmingham. She is fellow of Academy of Social Sciences, the UK. Her main research interests span multilingual and intercultural communication and child language.

1 Introduction: Are Discourse Analysts 'Essential Workers'?

Rodney H. Jones

When I was in the first grade, the teacher asked us to stand up one by one and tell the class what our fathers did. This was 1965, and so questions about what our mothers did rarely came up. I watched all my classmates declare proudly that their fathers were postmen, or firemen, or construction workers. Then it was my turn and I had to explain that my father was a public relations man (again, it was 1965, and so names of professions were still gendered – there were no 'public relations people' or 'public relations professionals'). My classmates stared back at me blankly: there were no pictures of public relations men alongside the firemen, police officers, teachers and shopkeepers in our primary school reader. But there was nothing I could do to clear things up for them. Truth be told, at that age I really had no idea what my father did. At that moment I resolved that, when I grew up, I would be something that people had heard of, a doctor or a fireman. As it turned out, I grew up to become a discourse analyst. So that didn't work out too well.

Of course, as I grew older, I did come to understand what my father did, and he came to understand what I did too. We used to say that his job was spinning things and my job was unspinning them. And we both knew that underlying what we both did was a conviction that words are important, that words have power, that words are things that ought to be handled with care.

Last month my father died of COVID-19, and suddenly words were not enough. He was in the USA and I was 4,000 miles away in the UK, and so our last conversations were sketchy video calls, first with him struggling to hold the phone up to his face, and later with the palliative care nurse propping an iPad in front of him for our final family Zoom calls. And in those calls, both of us, probably for the first time in our lives were at a loss for words, he because he could hardly breathe, and I because I didn't know what to say. There was no amount of unspinning that could help me make sense of what was happening. Sure, I could deconstruct the president's rhetoric on coronavirus or the way it was covered on Fox News, which my father watched religiously, but all that faded into the background. I could say the things I was *supposed* to say, the words that experts had decided were what you should say to a dying person. 'I love you.' 'I forgive you.' 'Forgive me.' But the words didn't seem to be enough. This was real.

I've been thinking a lot during lockdown about what I do. I guess a lot of people have. The coronavirus pandemic has brought into sharp relief which of us are 'essential workers' (here in the UK they call them 'key workers') and which of us aren't, revealing the ironic fact that those who do the most essential jobs like stocking supermarket shelves and delivering packages for Amazon often get paid the least. It has also made clear the distinction between those of us who can work from home, and those (like the doctor and the fireman that I never became) who have to venture out every day into a virus-ridden world. So it's gotten me to consider whether what I'm doing with my life is 'essential' or not, which is probably something all of us would do well to consider from time to time.

My colleagues and I started the blog Viral Discourse (https://viraldiscourse .com), where early drafts of the essays in this Element were first published, in the midst of the pandemic, partly to keep track of what we were thinking, how we were making sense of what was going on around us, and partly to help us make sense of what we do, to help us figure out the different ways being a discourse analyst is relevant to the current moment. After a while, we came to the decision that we wanted to turn these short pieces into a more permanent document of our experiences, one which brought together our different perspectives in a way that we imagined would be useful for students of discourse analysis and for scholars in the humanities and social sciences struggling to respond to this crisis and to future crises.

Can Discourse Analysis Save Lives?

Two decades ago, in the midst of the George W. Bush's War on Terror, my now-deceased mentor Ron Scollon wrote an essay called 'What's the point? Can mediated discourse analysis stop the war?' (Scollon, 2002). We might ask a similar question. Can discourse analysis stop the deaths? Or stop people – whether they be politicians or the people around us – from doing things that seem to be increasing the death toll? But maybe that's the wrong question. Maybe the question should be more along the lines of, what can discourse analysis do to help us live with death, to communicate about those things that are happening to us just a little bit better, and to understand the power of words to infect and to heal, and to learn how to treat them with care?

That's pretty much the conclusion Ron came to as well. The real question, he decided, was not whether or not he could stop the war, but rather something a bit less dramatic and maybe a bit more important. 'What can I do,' he wrote, 'that neither abdicates all action and responsibility to those who are causing such enormous human devastation nor quixotically burns up my life and the lives of those around me trying to feel as if we are taking meaningful action?'

The kind of discourse analysis Ron did – mediated discourse analysis – is all about 'meaningful actions', or rather, about understanding how every action is meaningful, and made possible by *meaning* (or discourse). Everything that happens is the result of chains of little actions following one after another, sometimes leading to monumental results, sometimes not, all woven together with words (and pictures, and other ways of making meaning). For Ron, the whole point of discourse analysis is to understand the role that discourse has in stitching together those chains of action, the role discourse has in making things happen, or not happen.

Like wars, epidemics – diseases of all kinds– are sites where these chains of action and meaning can get particularly knotty and hard to untangle. One reason for this, as I argued in my 2013 book about health communication, is this:

> Talking about health in any context is a complicated thing, first because when one is talking about health one is usually talking about other things as well, things like fear, trust, commitment, love, money, morality, politics and death, just to name a few. Second, communicating about health can be used to accomplish many different social actions from making an insurance claim, to making love, to making conversation around the dinner table, and how one talks about it depends on what one is doing with the talk. (Jones, 2013: 3)

Two decades ago, in the midst of a different pandemic, the cultural critic Paula Treichler (1999: 11) called AIDS an 'epidemic of signification'. 'Try as we may to treat AIDS as an "infectious disease" and nothing more,' she wrote, 'meanings continue to multiply wildly.' AIDS had become 'a chaotic assemblage of understandings' – or, as Ron might have put it, a knot of entangled chains of discourse and action – a 'horrendously complex entity made up of linkages among very different and independent discourses and ideologies, semiotic systems and their signs' (Scollon, 2002). 'We cannot,' Treichler (1999: 11) concluded, 'look "through" language to determine what AIDS "really" is. Rather we must look *at* language. We must *intervene at the point where meaning is created.*'

Noticing

In the end of the day, the best thing about discourse analysis is that it provides us with frameworks to notice when and how meaning is created, and sometimes to productively intervene. Each short research note in this Element might be seen as a window into that process of noticing – an example of a discourse analyst zeroing in on some point where meaning was created around the pandemic at some particular moment in some particular place, whether it be noticing the signs pasted in the windows of shuttered shops in our neighbourhood, or the slogans the prime minister was decorating his lectern with for his coronavirus briefings, or the metaphors used to talk about the pandemic in the newspapers, or the videos, memes and hashtags that shot through our social media feeds. And what they end up noticing is that making meaning in the context of COVID-19 is never just about COVID-19, but also about things like inequality, racism, militarism, cultural identity, expertise, and power, and sometimes meaning itself; what they end up noticing is how, at times like this, it is not just meaning but also 'ambiguity and uncertainty' that need to be 'socially and linguistically managed' (Treichler 1999: 16).

One thing these essays remind us is that it is the *particularity* of these points where meaning is created that is most important – that meaning is *always* situated, that it is always created in some place, at some time, at some point in a chain of actions. The same words have different meanings depending on whether or not they appear on our social media feeds or come from the mouth of the prime minister. And so these analyses are also necessarily situated. They were written in the midst of the pandemic by people who were experiencing it in all of the big and small ways that others were.

Each of these pieces, then, is an example of discourse analysis being done *in vivo*, an attempt to make sense of what was happening as it happened. In some of them, we have plucked out some pieces of data from the stream of events and tried to test out our analytical apparatus on it, hoping to derive some insight or some foothold for future research. In others we have attempted to build a preliminary theoretical framework around what we were witnessing, a skeleton of concepts that might later be applied to more carefully collected data. And so the ideas presented here are necessarily tentative, snapshots of our thinking at particular points in a quickly changing narrative. In one sense, that might be a weakness. Couldn't we have waited until we had more data, more certainty, something more 'substantial' to share? But in another sense, it is their incompleteness that is their strength, the glimpses they offer into how we as discourse analysts were making sense of things day by day; day by day trying to figure out what it means to be 'essential'.

By the time this Element is published, the contours of the pandemic and people's responses to it will no doubt have changed, and by the time some readers read this, the pandemic will be a distant memory. Hopefully. We will also have moved on in our thinking. We might have followed the threads we have picked up here, developing these ideas into more substantial projects, grant applications or research articles, or we might have moved on to different things. But what we wanted to capture here were those initial moments of sense making, when discourse analysts start to notice things and begin to map out where they want to go.

Another strength of this small volume is the range of different perspectives for understanding meaning and action that are represented. We are all discourse analysts, but we have our own tribes and our own tricks. These 'bags of tricks' go by names like critical discourse analysis, multimodal discourse analysis, mediated discourse analysis, social semiotics, interactional sociolinguistics, genre analysis, linguistic landscape studies and corpus-assisted discourse analysis. Some readers will be familiar with these various frameworks, and others less so. Where possible, the authors have tried to provide a short explanation of the main principles guiding their analysis and to use their analysis or theoretical discussion to illustrate how these principles might be applied. For this reason, this collection is suitable not just for seasoned discourse analysts, but also for those just getting started in the field.

None of the short essays in this Element are going to save anyone's life. I'm pretty sure of that. But they might play some small part in some chain of action that ends up saving someone's life, or making someone's life better, or helping someone talk to someone who refuses to wear a face mask without getting into an argument, or getting someone to think twice about retweeting that hateful COVID-related tweet. More importantly, they might help us become more sensitive to those chains of action that have been set into motion by this virus and the role discourse plays in them before we get too entangled in them, before they get wrapped around us so tightly that we can't talk. They might get us closer to understanding how to productively intervene where meaning is created. They might contribute, somewhere down the line, to the construction of a new architecture for understanding how to talk to each other over seemingly irresolvable physical and ideological distances in contexts where we are reduced to tiny iPhone-sized faces. They might in some small way help us to figure out what it means to be essential to the people around us, and how to say the things that need saying at the moments they need saying and in the ways they need saying; things like 'I love you', 'I forgive you', 'Forgive me'.

2 The Veil of Civilization and the Semiotics of the Mask

Rodney H. Jones

Since the start of the pandemic, there has been a dramatic shift in the debate about wearing face masks to slow the spread of the coronavirus. In the beginning, most East Asian governments and even some European ones such as Austria and the Czech republic came down on the side of face masks. But the initial response in the United States and the United Kingdom were anti-mask. In these countries, experts were deployed to question the quality of the 'evidence' regarding the efficacy of masks (see Hafner, Section 3). There were those who worried that many people didn't know how to wear masks properly, and some even insisted that wearing masks would actually make people *more* vulnerable to infection.

At that time in the UK and the USA, wearing a surgical mask in public, especially if you looked East Asian, could even invite racist attacks, a phenomenon that *The Guardian* dubbed 'maskphobia' (Weale, 2020). At the same time, there were also reports of Westerners in Asian locales receiving similar abuse for *not* wearing face masks (Choi, 2020). A piece of graffiti on the streets of Hong Kong in March declared: 'HEY *YOU GWEILO*! Are you too poor to buy a mask?' (*gweilo* being a less than flattering Cantonese term for foreigner).

In the UK, not all of the anti-mask sentiment directed towards East Asians was violent. Some of it was well meaning. At one UK university, a British Professor insisted that a Chinese student take her mask off during class. 'I have to see your face,' he said, and then proceeded to 'educate' her about why masks are 'unscientific'. A few days later, the vice-chancellor of the same university sent a message to staff and students reminding them that, while there was 'no evidence' that people should wear masks, for some people mask wearing was part of their 'culture', and so should be 'tolerated'.

But, even when experts were telling them not to, as the epidemic started to take hold in their countries, many people in the USA and UK started buying up masks. For some it seemed that their governments' anti-mask messages were designed more to manage the scarcity of masks than to actually protect people. In mid-March, sociologist Zeynap Tufekci (2020) argued in the *New York Times* that 'the top-down conversation around masks has become a case study in how not to communicate with the public, especially now that the traditional gatekeepers like media and health authorities have much less control'. Tufekci's criticism of anti-mask messages focused mostly on how they ignored the complex flows of information around health and risk in contemporary societies. But there is also a more discourse-analytical critique to be made, one which shows how the difficulties with communicating about face masks is also a result of ignoring the complex nature of *meaning*.

Much work in discourse analysis owes a debt to the older field of semiotics, pioneered by Charles Peirce in the mid nineteenth century. The focus of semiotics is not just *what* signs mean, but *how* they mean – the various ways that objects, utterances and inscriptions get entangled with ideas, people and social relationships. In the 1980s, linguists Robert Hodge and Gunther Kress (1988) drew on this tradition to formulate an approach they called *social semiotics*. One important focus of this approach has been the strategic ways people combine different kinds of semiotic resources for particular purposes (see Ho, Section 4). An equally important focus has been understanding how the 'meaning potential' of different resources changes as society changes, and how resources come to us 'heavy' with the histories of their past uses. Sign systems are, as Halliday (1978) pointed out, ultimately *functional*, ultimately reflections of the societies that invent them, the kinds of things people in those societies need to do and the kinds of relationships they have with one another.

Masks are objects that come to us particularly heavy with meanings, meanings that can change depending on the social contexts in which masks are worn. Masks are never just one thing. They are always at least three kinds of things at one time. They are things that *conceal*, things that *protect* and things that *transform*. And understanding this can help us to make sense of how the discourse around masks has changed, and how it's likely to change in the future.

Masks as Things That Conceal

One of the most important functions of masks throughout history has been *to conceal* the face of the wearer – either in order to hide their identity, or to perform modesty or decorum. Masks are the accessories of bandits and bank robbers, but nuns and brides also often appear veiled. How masks are used as coverings reveals societal beliefs about what should and what shouldn't be covered in different circumstances. An example of this can be seen in the aforementioned professor's insistence to his Chinese student, that, in the classroom, 'I need to see your face'. In Christian moral philosophy and Western culture more generally, there has always been a suspicion of masks, as they function to disjoin identity from behaviour, making people essentially *unaccountable*.

In the Muslim tradition, of course, there are different beliefs about the meaning of a covered face. The purpose of veiling a woman's face is not to conceal her evil intentions, but to discourage male onlookers from developing their own. Obviously, the unease of Europeans and Americans with East Asians wearing masks during the pandemic has been nothing compared to their long-standing discomfort with Islamic women wearing veils (niqabs, burkas), and just as 'rational arguments' were central to anti-face-mask rhetoric, 'rational arguments' about social order have been used against the veil. Justifications for France's 2010 law making it an offence to 'wear clothing designed to conceal one's face', for instance, do not normally single out Islamic women, but rather focus on how the act of concealing one's face constitutes a danger to public safety and public order.

Not surprisingly, this law ended up being used by scammers to target mask-wearing Chinese during the early days of the pandemic, with people in Paris pretending to be police officers stopping masked Chinese tourists and fining them €250 for violating the French anti-mask law. Perhaps the most ironic turn of events, though, was when Chinese students in the UK started wearing burkas to conceal their surgical masks in order to avoid harassment, apparently calculating that coronavirus related 'maskphobia' in the UK exceeded Islamophobia.

Masks as Things that Protect

Another central function of masks is to protect their wearers against magic spells, bad luck, air pollution, tear gas or diseases. In many cultures, masks have been endowed with the power to ward off evil spirits. Halloween masks, in fact, are linked to the 'guises' worn for the ancient Celtic festival of Samhain to protect wearers from malevolent ghosts. As with its concealing function, the protective function of the mask provides a window into principles upon which societies organize social relationships and their understandings of the nature of personhood. The protective function of masks turns them into a tool for distinguishing between good and evil, between inside and outside and between you and me.

This is just as true in the current debate around the ability of face masks to protect against the coronavirus as it was in the ancient rituals of the Celts. The striking thing about the European and American guidelines about mask wearing that were in place in the early days of the pandemic is the degree to which they focused on *the wearer* of the mask as the one who is (or is not) protected. For example:

> **USA**
> Centers for Disease Control and Prevention does not recommend that people who are well wear a face mask (including respirators) to *protect themselves* from respiratory diseases, including COVID-19.
> **UK**
> Face masks play a very important role in places such as hospitals, but there is very little evidence of widespread *benefit for members of the public*.

This contrasts with the advice of the Hong Kong Department of Health, which states:

> Surgical masks can prevent *transmission of respiratory viruses from people who are ill*. It is essential for people who are symptomatic (even if they have mild symptoms) to wear a surgical mask.

In Asia, wearing masks has always been a matter of protecting other people. Primary school students are taught to wear masks when they have a cold, and in times of epidemics, masks serve as a visible reminder that limiting infection is everyone's civic responsibility.

'Civic responsibility' was also a trope in anti-mask discourses in the West. In the UK, for instance, in the beginning of the pandemic, the way to signal virtue, was to *not* wear a mask in order to save them for healthcare workers – to 'protect the NHS'. One problem with this sloganeering was that it took attention away from the neoliberal policies, including the decade of austerity imposed on the NHS by the Tories, that led to shortages of personal protective equipment in the first place.

Masks as Things that Transform

According to anthropologists, the most important function of masks is not to conceal the face of the wearer nor to protect them from harm, but to *transform* them. This is what happens when superheroes don masks – they are transformed from ordinary beings to extraordinary beings. The usual way of thinking about this transformation, however, is in terms of *representational* meaning. The mask transforms its wearer into the being – say an animal or a god – whose face is represented on the mask. Such transformations are necessarily temporary. When the wearer takes off the mask, he or she returns to being human.

But anthropologist Donald Pollock (1995) proposes that a more important aspect of this transformation has to do with what semioticians and linguists call *indexical* meaning, the kind of meaning that is made when certain signs over time become associated with certain kinds of people, places, activities or values. In sociolinguistics, for example, certain ways of speaking can come to *index* certain regions, classes or kinds of people. When we see the transformative power of masks as a matter of indexical meaning, we come to see how meaning is socially constructed over time and reflects larger constellations of power and ideology within a society.

Another anthropologist, Christos Lynteris (2018), traces the practice of East Asians wearing face masks to the Great Manchurian Plague Epidemic of 1910–11, which broke out while the Chinese, Japanese, Russians and missionaries from Europe and America were vying for influence over the region. In the midst of this struggle, Wu Liande, a Chinese doctor in Harbin, defied the conventional wisdom of foreign experts by suggesting that, unlike earlier manifestations of plague, this strain was airborne. To protect people from infection, Wu invented an 'anti-plague mask' (Fig. 2.1), meant to be worn not just by doctors and patients but also their contacts, and, if possible, *by the entire population* of the region.

The Europeans were dismissive of the mask, not just because they were sceptical of Wu's airborne contagion theory, but also because they were sceptical that Chinese doctors had the level of 'civilization' required to understand science. Among Dr Wu's most fervent opponents was the distinguished French physician Dr Gérald Mesny. In his autobiography, Wu related in the third person one of his confrontations with Mesny.

> Dr. Wu was seated in a large padded armchair, trying to smile away their differences. The Frenchman was excited, and kept on walking to and fro in the heated room. Suddenly, unable to contain himself any longer, he faced Dr. Wu, raised both his arms in a threatening manner, and with bulging eyes cried out 'You, you Chinaman, how dare you laugh at me and contradict your superior?' (Wu, 1959: 19)

Not long after this meeting, Mesny visited plague hospitals without wearing Wu's mask, quickly contracted the disease and died, leading other foreign doctors as well as the general public to quickly adopt the mask.

The main point of Lynteris's article is not to reveal how the arrogance and racism of Europeans prevented them from adopting a life-saving technology, but rather the way Wu's mask acted to *transform* the identities of Chinese doctors and unsettle the existing relationships of power. The mask came

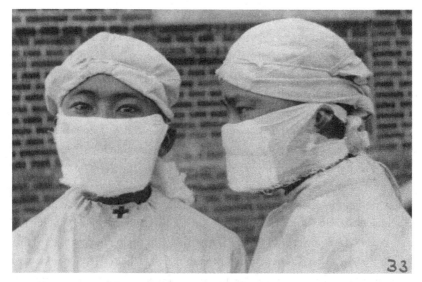

Figure 2.1 Doctors in Harbin wearing 'anti-plague' masks (University of Hong Kong Libraries)

to *index* not just medical rationalism but the ability of the Chinese to battle epidemics without the help of foreigners. It acted to transform the populous as well from 'a superstitious and ignorant' mass into an 'enlightened and hygienic-minded population' (Lynteris 2018): 451). The 'plague mask' functioned not just as a medical device, but as a 'veil of civilization'.

The role that medical masks took in the 'culture wars' of early twentieth century China echoes eerily through contemporary discussions of masks in which, like Mesny, conservative politicians use their refusal to wear masks as an assertion of power (and their followers use it as an expression of 'freedom'), some meeting with a similar fate as the French doctor. Nowadays, public health officials marvel that a simple public health measure like mask wearing has become 'political', but given the transformative power of masks, their power to index identities, political allegiances and even the idea of civilization itself, this is not at all surprising. As anthropologists would tell us, it is the transformative power of masks that makes them so magical, and so dangerous, that gives them the power to bring people together, and to tear them apart.

The Veil of Civilization

There has developed another way to talk about masks during this pandemic that goes beyond conceptions of right and wrong, good and evil, self and other: the discourse of masks as *gifts*. Like the mask, the gift is another favourite topic of anthropologists, among the most famous being Marcel Mauss (1966) who pointed out the importance of practices of gift giving in so-called 'archaic' societies for maintaining social cohesion and creating mutual trust between people. The power of the gift, Mauss says, lies in the way *reciprocity* supports generosity.

All crises give rise to heart-warming tales of heroism and generosity, and that's a good thing. Among the stories that went viral in the early days of the pandemic was the story of Dr Sarosh Ashraf Janjua, who got stopped for speeding while commuting to the hospital where she works in Minnesota. Instead of giving her a speeding ticket, the officer who stopped her gave her the store of N95 masks the state had given him for his protection. 'This complete stranger, who owed me nothing and is more on the front lines than I am,' she wrote on her Facebook page, 'shared his precious masks with me, without my even asking', and then added: 'The veil of civilization may be thin, but not all that lies behind it is savage ... We are going to be OK' (Boroff, 2020).

Less dramatic but equally meaningful are the countless stories of ordinary people forming sewing groups to make masks both for frontline workers and for the general public. What masks mean for people like this, many of them retired, is a chance to make a contribution in the face of the maddening paradox of people being 'mobilized' to 'stay at home'.

Even sharing things on social media, though sometimes dismissed as trivial, can prime people's orientation to generosity and reciprocity. An example is the hashtag #masks4all started by the Czech authorities, which encourages people to share Instagram photos of themselves wearing masks. It may not seem so important, but making masked faces something we share rather than something we argue about might be just what is needed, and the campaign's slogan: 'I protect you, you protect me', again, primes people to focus on reciprocity.

Cultivating the language of generosity and reciprocity, it seems to me, is especially important at a time when many politicians have chosen to talk about the crisis using the language of war (see Jaworska, Section 5), and, in places like the USA and the UK, masks have come to be seen as actual weapons in partisan 'culture wars', banners of people's political loyalties or objects with which to build conspiracy theories.

The way we have talked about masks during this crisis reveals some troubling cracks in the social, psychological and discursive equipment we need to deal with it: cracks in our tolerance, cracks in our healthcare and economic systems and cracks in our ability to negotiate common *meanings*. As sociologist Eric Klinenberg puts it:

> If there's ever been a moment where we needed to be unified – unified such that I decide to stay at home because I'm concerned about you and I'm concerned about us – a pandemic situation is that moment. It's a moment like this where we see the extent to which our fate is linked – where my well-being hinges on yours. (Klein, 2020)

In the end, masks alone won't save us. As Lynteris (2018: 452) puts it, masks are just fragile 'talismans' that allow humanity to 'persist on the edge of the end of the world'. The real veil of civilization lies in ourselves.

3 Communicating Expertise in the COVID-19 Pandemic: A Genre Analytical Perspective

Christoph A. Hafner

The initial stages of the COVID-19 pandemic presented an interesting moment for scientific and medical experts. The response at the beginning of 2020 was characterized by unprecedented measures, including government-mandated lockdowns of entire populations, imposed in a context of great uncertainty. At the time, knowledge of the virus and of the pandemic was sketchy at best. It was therefore not surprising that political leaders turned to scientific and medical experts for assistance, while the mainstream media solicited opinion articles and interviews from them on a diverse range of topics related to the pandemic. Many of these experts found themselves, quite suddenly, launched into prominence. People were suddenly listening to what they had to say. How did experts respond to the challenge of expressing themselves to this suddenly attentive public audience? What discursive strategies did they use?

These questions are important to investigate because part of being an expert is being able to communicate in just this kind of situation: an expert communicator can be called on to make specialist knowledge accessible to a non-specialist audience. At times, this can include 'engagement' and 'dialogue' with the general public (Stilgoe et al., 2014). When expert scientists communicate with public audiences, for example in written popular science articles, they often adopt a more 'accessible' and 'engaging' form of language (Hyland, 2010; Parkinson & Adendorff, 2004). In this section, I examine the discourse of such expert scientists as they communicate with a wider public through opinion articles in the mainstream media, focused especially on the issue of universal face mask use. This was an issue that emerged in the early stages of the COVID-19 pandemic and continued to be a source of political controversy at the time of writing in late 2020 (see also Ho, Section 4; Jones, Section XX).

In the analysis, I use tools of genre analysis (Bhatia, 1993, 2004; Hafner, 2010; Swales, 1990), which is an approach that examines the specialized discourse of members of professional discourse communities. Genres are situated, recurrent, 'communicative events' (Swales, 1990) that also have identifiable formal features: they follow particular expected rhetorical structures, making them recognizable to the intended audience and therefore more effective both as vehicles of communication and 'tools' of social action. Genres can therefore be seen as conventionalized ways of 'getting things done' with language. This means that they have a 'communicative purpose' and particular genres are, in part, defined by this common shared purpose. The mainstream media expert opinion article that forms the focus of this section is an example of a genre, with the communicative purpose of informing the general public of scientific knowledge and persuading them to take certain kinds of action.

As suggested, when expert professionals use genres to facilitate communication, they make use of expected organizational structures, grammatical forms and lexical features in order to achieve their social goals and their communicative purposes. But genre analysis goes deeper than this. It also shows how experts adopt specialized ways of thinking and reasoning, presenting a certain kind of professional, expert identity through their texts (Dressen-Hammouda, 2008; Hafner, 2013). Among other things, genre analysis therefore seeks to draw connections between the formal features of the genres that experts make use of and the ways of thinking and being that underlie them. In the following analysis, I show how, using particular discursive forms, the scientific experts examined align themselves with the valued ways of thinking and being of their professional discourse communities, even as they write for a lay, public audience. The analysis also shows how they do this in different ways and to a greater or lesser extent, likely reflecting ideological choices made in the service of the particular goals of individual scientists.

What Counts as Evidence? Universal Face Mask Use in the COVID-19 Crisis

In the initial stages of the global pandemic, there was no clear scientific or policy consensus on whether it would be beneficial for whole populations to adopt face masks (see Jones, Section 2). While the World Health Organization (WHO) initially counselled against universal face mask use, in April 2020 the WHO changed its advice and recommended it (Ting, 2020). At the same time, different governments around the world adopted noticeably different official policies, all the while claiming that they were following scientific advice. How was it possible for different members of the scientific community to reach such radically different positions? How did these experts justify their different stances and communicate them to the public? I will seek to answer such questions by analysing two articles that appeared in the Guardian on 2 and 3 April 2020, and that featured the views of expert professionals. These are:

- Face masks: can they slow coronavirus spread – and should we be wearing them? (2 April 2020) (Renwick, 2020): A panel of four experts answer questions on the pros and cons of face mask use, coming out in favour of it. Here I consider a comment by Jeremy Howard, Distinguished Research Scientist, University of San Francisco and founder of the #Masks4All campaign.
- Do face masks protect against coronavirus? Here's what scientists know so far (3 April 2020) (Heymann, 2020): David Heymann, Professor of Infectious Disease Epidemiology, London School of Hygiene & Tropical Medicine,

asks 'what does the evidence say about how well face masks work, and who should wear them?' He concludes that there is an absence of evidence for the effectiveness of mask use by the general public.

These articles were selected because they occurred at a critical moment in the mainstream media discourse on the pandemic: they exemplify scientists attempting communication with the public in an area of significant urgency and uncertainty. So much uncertainty, in fact, that scientists were in clear public disagreement with one another, as the analysis shows. For the purposes of this article, the small data set allows for an in-depth comparison of generic strategies in this critical moment. A larger data set would shed further light on the predictive power of the analysis to identify conventionalized patterns of performing expert identities in this context.

Knowns and Unknowns (Howard)

In the 2 April article, Howard is asked: 'Is there any way to disaggregate the widespread use of face masks from other measures – like social distancing – to understand how effective they are?' Here is his full response:

> We absolutely can't. There are four measures – rigorous testing, contact tracing, quarantine of potentially infected persons and universal mask-wearing – that represent a *known* good recipe. *We don't know* exactly which combination of those things works and how important each one is. We've just got to do what works. (Example 1, emphasis added)

The response begins with an interesting use of the first person plural pronoun 'we', referring either to the scientific community, or more inclusively, to the community as a whole. Howard references both 'knowns' and 'unknowns'. He talks about a 'known good recipe' that includes universal mask use but also notes that 'we don't know' how important, say, universal face mask use is as an ingredient in that mix. He omits providing any evidence for the 'known good recipe', either taking this for granted or assuming that readers will supply it for themselves. Interestingly, while he references uncertainties (unknowns), Howard does so *in a direct and certain manner*, avoiding any reliance on epistemic modality or hedging devices.

Absence of Evidence (Heymann)

In the 3 April article, Heymann (Fig. 3.1) provides a longer, more nuanced view of available scientific knowledge. The article begins by reviewing what we know we can do in response to COVID-19, then reviews what the evidence says about face masks, and concludes by considering what we should now do. In this

Figure 3.1 With the COVID-19 crisis, expert professionals like David Heymann have been called on to explain the situation to the public. (Image (CC BY 2.0) by Don Pollard/Council on Foreign Relations, Chatham House on Flickr)

last section, he lists one possible reason for the public wearing masks ('as a precaution') and four possible reasons why the public might not.

In this article, the notion of 'evidence' plays an important role. For example, here is how the writer characterizes existing measures, not including mask use:

> We know *from scientific evidence*, as well as what we have learned from other countries further ahead in their epidemics, that these things work. (Example 2, emphasis added)

Here is how he presents knowledge about face mask use:

> There is *a lack of good, robust evidence* on the effectiveness of standard face masks worn by the public. (Example 3, emphasis added)

> *We don't even have good, case-controlled studies* about how effective face masks are at preventing the spread of influenza, which is the model for respiratory virus diseases. There have been some studies comparing a group of people who got flu with a group of people who didn't get flu, which asked retrospectively whether they wore face masks, but *they don't convincingly tell us* that it was the face mask, rather than something else, that was effective in preventing transmission of flu. (Example 4, emphasis added)

Example 4 is also interesting because the writer also notes *limitations* in existing scientific studies, noting that the evidence is not convincing.

Different Standards of Evidence?

Howard and Heymann seem to be using different standards of evidence and this leads them to adopt a fundamentally different stance on the issue of universal face mask use. Heymann makes the standard explicit when he says:

> One of the best forms of evidence in medical research is a randomised controlled trial. ... We would have difficulty doing this kind of trial of face masks, because it's impossible for participants to be unaware of whether or not they're wearing a mask. (Example 5)

Even though both scientists make claims about what is known and unknown, their basis for doing so is different. While not made explicit, Howard is apparently relying on the experience to date of countries fighting the coronavirus to support the need for universal mask use. Meanwhile, Heymann relies on the lack of randomized controlled trials to establish that there is an absence of 'robust evidence' for this kind of mask use. Yet, at the same time, Heymann does cite 'what we have learned from other countries further ahead in their epidemics' when approving other methods like social distancing. This suggests the possibility that ideological considerations could influence the standard of evidence that is applied. Here, different standards of evidence are apparently *used strategically* to allow for the promotion of particular individual goals. This is an example of what Bhatia (2004) characterizes as the strategic use of generic conventions to realize 'private intentions'. In the political arena, we might therefore see different kinds of scientific evidence being deployed to justify different political positions.

Even if Heymann's stance in the 3 April article did not seem very sympathetic to the universal use of face masks, this stance may have subsequently changed. In a 2 April BBC interview[1], he appears more open to the possibility that masks could be effective, saying

> it might be that wearing a mask is equally as effective or more effective than distancing, provided that mask is worn properly and provided that people don't infect themselves when they're taking the mask off and touch an outer surface which may be contaminated. (Example 6)

Here it's interesting how carefully he presents this position, using a raft of 'hedging devices' (e.g. 'it might be', 'provided that', 'may be'; see Hyland, 2005) to refrain from committing entirely to the position. Heymann is careful here to present the state of knowledge as uncertain and avoid a black-and-white 'answer'.

---

[1] The fact that the interview was aired before the opinion article could be printed exemplifies the speed at which this debate was unfolding.

Conclusions

A lack of consensus in expert scientific knowledge is nothing new. New knowledge emerges and is 'perfected' when scientists identify and address pre-existing gaps by applying rigorous scientific procedures. What we see in the analysis is that, at least in the context of mainstream media articles, the scientific reasoning process can be underpinned by different kinds of evidence, which would be considered to be more or less rigorous according to the conventions of the professional scientific community. These evidential standards might not be spelled out at all (as was the case with Howard), or the same scientist could, wittingly or unwittingly, use different standards in different domains (as was the case with Heymann). The analysis shows that scientific arguments can be marshalled to support conflicting policy choices, so that ultimately the stance adopted could have more to do with ideological considerations than with scientific reasons. In addition, the lack of a unified stance is of course likely to hamper any effort to persuade the public to take concrete action, like wearing or not wearing a mask.

At the same time, the strategic and potentially biased use of discourse to construct expert knowledge may be especially difficult for lay audiences, outsiders to the scientific community, to detect. This is because of the way that it relies on taken-for-granted mental models, the ways of thinking that are considered acceptable in the making of scientific claims. Understanding these expert knowledge constructions therefore calls for a critical evaluation of the evidence that underlies them based on an understanding of the procedures that were used to generate that evidence. In developing this understanding, a genre analytical approach has a lot to offer because it sees language and discourse as intimately bound up with the modes of reasoning employed by particular expert professional cultures. However, in this case, even such a critical reading may not have been sufficient to get at the heart of the matter. The debate that I have described here was framed purely as a matter of scientific knowledge and understanding. Yet, as is widely acknowledged, a key ingredient in policy advice against universal mask use was the fact that personal protective equipment for health care workers was in short supply at the time (see Jones, Section 2). While this policy consideration does not form part of the scientific analysis, it may well have had an impact on it.

4 Face Masks and Cultural Identity on YouTube
Wing Yee Jenifer Ho
Face Masks on YouTube

Unlike hand washing, about which there is unanimous agreement of its effectiveness in fighting coronavirus, the practice of wearing face masks has, in many countries, become a complex *moral* question about civic responsibility and altruism. Although the attitude towards face masks has changed considerably in recent months, as more people recognized their effectiveness in curbing the spread of the virus, the debate over whether to mask or not is not yet settled. This section focuses on the early days of the pandemic, from March to April 2020, when there was still considerable skepticism in many places concerning the use of face masks. The question of whether to mask or not has been interpreted by some as evidence of 'cultural' differences between East Asians and Europeans /Americans, or taken as an opportunity to position some cultures as more 'sensible', 'scientific' or 'socially responsible' than others. One place where this 'cultural positioning' is evident is in YouTube videos. The positioning of the 'prepared' (i.e. the masked) and the 'unprepared' (i.e. the unmasked) has been a dominant discourse in a considerable number of videos posted on YouTube. Among these videos, some are created by Chinese-speaking users who film their lives under quarantine, often in their home countries (mostly in Europe or in the United States). This section focuses on one such video and examines how a multilingual language user identity is seen as aligning with the masking practice, and how this becomes a digitally mediated cultural performance. In my analysis, I unpack how cultural positioning between the 'East' and the 'West' on the topic of face masks is constructed, drawing on the concepts of *multimodality* and *translanguaging*, both of which highlight the multimodal and multilingual nature of communication in the contemporary world, particularly in digitally mediated communication.

Multimodality and Translanguaging

Multimodality is an approach which recognizes the fact that communication involves more than just the use of language. Communication is inherently *multimodal*; that is, multiple modes such as images, sound, colour, gesture, proxemics, to name a few, work together in multimodal ensembles to make meaning (Kress, 2010). This section employs a *social semiotic approach* to multimodality to examine how multimodal resources are orchestrated by the sign-maker to make meaning which expresses the sign-maker's interest in the world.

Translanguaging is an analytical approach to multilingual language users' fluid language practices. It refers to 'the deployment of a speaker's full linguistic repertoire without regard for watchful adherence to the socially and politically defined boundaries of named (and usually national and state) languages' (Otheguy et al., 2015: 283). A translanguaging perspective emphasizes the fact that multilingual speakers, or even the so-called monolingual speakers, go beyond the artificial divide of the so-called linguistic, paralinguistic and the extralinguistic dimensions of communication as they orchestrate their meaning- and sense-making resources, demonstrating creativity and criticality (Li, 2011; 2018).

Whilst multimodality emphasizes the multiplicity of modes used in communication, and how they function as ensembles to make meaning, the notion of translanguaging allows us to focus on knowledge construction, or in the case of this section, *cultural positioning*, which goes beyond linguistic structures, script systems and modalities (Li Wei, 2018). Translanguaging is a process of mobilizing one's repertoire, which serves as a record of one's life experiences and mobility (Blommaert & Backus, 2013). This integrated framework not only offers a socio-historical and cultural dimension to our understanding of multimodal and multilingual practices, it also shifts attention from analysis of texts to moment-by-moment unfolding of interactions which focuses on individual language users' multilingual and multimodal repertoire.

Teacher Mike's 'America Quarantine Vlog'

This section examines a video from a series featuring an American who calls himself *Teacher Mike*. Teacher Mike lived in China before returning to the United States shortly before he filmed the video. He regularly posts videos of his daily life under quarantine, and he also teaches English to a predominantly Chinese audience. Teacher Mike is fluent in Mandarin Chinese, and most of his videos about his life under quarantine are produced in Mandarin Chinese. The video featured in this section documents his visit to a supermarket in the United States. It was uploaded to YouTube on 29 April 2020. This was the time when the use of face coverings was broadly encouraged by experts in the USA.

The video (Video 4.1) starts with Teacher Mike showing viewers his empty fridge, which leads to his supermarket trip. He is shown driving to the supermarket and walking into the supermarket, and by that time he is already wearing a face mask and a pair of gloves. Inside the supermarket, he shows the items that he plans to buy, and in the process, he counts how many people in the supermarket are not wearing masks or any kind of face covering.

From an analytical standpoint, this process of counting is seen as significant, as it expresses the position that the video-creator takes regarding the use of face masks in public spaces like supermarkets. This example is also selected because it showcases how different resources orchestrate to help Teacher Mike construct a position with regards to face masks. The following analysis focuses on

Teacher Mike shopping in the supermarket, which lasts for just over two minutes. I follow the procedure of 'moment analysis' outlined in Li (2011: 1223) which '[highlights] the spontaneous performances of the multilingual language users, and the consequences of the spontaneous performances for the individuals concerned and for the translanguaging space'. The transcription system used here is a modified version of previous works on multimodal text and interaction analysis (see e.g. Ho & Li, 2019; Li & Ho, 2018) which attends to the temporal and modal unfolding of the event.

As Teacher Mike enters the supermarket (Fig. 4.1), he comments that he feels safe because most people in the supermarket are wearing masks and gloves. At this very moment, he has already indicated his alignment with face masks linguistically, using fluent Chinese to address the audience. He places his camera in a shopping trolley and he pays attention to both his immediate physical environment (i.e. the supermarket aisles, the products on the shelves), and the people around him. At the same time, he talks directly to the audience, which is signaled by his gaze which alternates between the camera and his surroundings (02:35). The combination of these modes gives the impression that he is taking the viewers on a grocery shopping trip as participants.

From 03:04 onwards until 03:55 (Figs. 4.2 and 4.3), he displays to the camera (and therefore, to his audience), each item that he puts into the trolley and notes the price of each item. During this very short period of time, whenever he sees anyone without a mask, the colour of the screen changes from maximum colour saturation to black and white (03:55). This corresponds to what Kress and van Leeuwen (2006) refer to as a change of modality, which constitutes a 'joint product of the judgements' between the sign-maker and the audience of whether something is represented as true or not (Ravelli & van Leeuwen, 2018). Modality depends on whether an image resembles what we would see in reality (Ravelli & van Leeuwen, 2018). This change in the representation of modality is salient, as the

Time	Speech*	Text on screen* (subtitles)	Screen-capture	Sound effect	Camera angle	Gaze
02:35	一進去就看到每個人都是戴口罩，都是戴手套，所以我放心了一點，因為感覺他們都是很看重這個疫情的情況。就是比較安全的。 *As I enter, everyone is wearing masks and gloves. I feel reassured, because it looks like they are treating this pandemic seriously. It feels quite safe.*	/	 	Soft background music	Low angle	Alternates between the immediate physical environment and the camera

Figure 4.1 Teacher Mike enters the supermarket (02:35)

Time	Speech*	Text on screen* (subtitles)	Screen-capture	Sound effect	Camera angle	Gaze
03:04	/	啤酒香腸 $2.99 (美金) *Bratwurst $2.99 (USD)*		Soft background music	Eye-level	/

Figure 4.2 Placing items in the shopping trolley

Time	Speech*	Text on screen* (subtitles)	Screen-capture	Sound effect	Camera angle	Gaze
03:05	/	沒戴口罩! *No mask on!*		Soft background music + Sound effect	Eye-level	/

Figure 4.3 The 'face mask moment'

change from maximum colour saturation to black and white seems to suggest a change in the 'truth value' of a given scene, and this truth value is co-constructed by both the sign-maker and the viewers. Based on the modality scale proposed by Kress and van Leeuwen (2006), images in black and white have the lowest modality. This change in colour saturation is used to depict scenes of people not wearing a face mask. Whilst it may be difficult to interpret this change in modality in isolation, if we turn our attention to the other modes, it may help us understand this particular scene in its entirety. Visually, next to the person seen without a mask, a big, red title in Chinese is superimposed on the frame which reads '沒戴口罩!' (No mask on!), accompanied by an arrow pointing directly at the person without a mask. The caption is accompanied by a special sound effect that interrupts the soft background music which reminds one of the sounds produced by computer games when players make the wrong move or provide the wrong answer. This orchestration of modes, including the use of language, image, sound and modality, all suggest a kind of cultural positioning associated with masking in supermarkets, which seems to be something along the lines of 'it is wrong to go to the supermarket without a mask'.

This can also be understood in light of Teacher Mike's background as a teacher. The choice of the colour red, together with the sound effect indicating a wrong answer, the red arrow pointing at the person in question, all align with his identity as a teacher. Here, Teacher Mike mobilizes the semiotic resources commonly used in pedagogic contexts when creating this video, which can be seen as a kind of 'resemiotization' – the process through which there is a shift in meaning as actions are redesigned from one mode to another (Iedema, 2003). This is also an instance of creativity whereby Teacher Mike pushes and breaks boundaries between pedagogic practices and everyday practices. This mobilization constitutes a kind of translangauging whereby language users '[go] beyond not only the boundaries between different-named languages but also linguistic codes, transcending modalities and making use of the technological environment and artifacts' (Ho & Li Wei, 2019: 533).

Multimodal Construction of Cultural Positioning

Teacher Mike's cultural positioning, particularly in regard to masking and social distancing, is constructed by a strategic orchestration of a range of modes: speech, writing, visuals, sound, camera angle and gaze. Whilst language (spoken and written) plays a role in expressing Teacher Mike's alignment with mask-wearing, a large part of the meaning is carried by other 'non-linguistic' modes, such as sound and gaze. The multimodal nature of communication thus warrants examination not only of what is spoken or written, but of the whole multimodal ensemble as we try to understand (digitally mediated) communicative practices. In particular, we need to understand the *orchestration* of these modes and describe how multilingual and multimodal semiotic systems work together (Zhu Hua et al., 2017). Had the modes been studied in isolation, it would not have been possible to understand the meaning that emerged from this configuration of modes.

Over the course of the pandemic, countries in East Asia have often been perceived as 'better prepared', one reason being that they are more receptive to the wearing of face masks (Chan, 2020). This alignment with face masks in Asia indexes 'preparedness' and 'knowledge'. This video is only one of many videos featuring Europeans or Americans speaking Chinese (Mandarin or other dialects) to talk about their experience related to the COVID-19 pandemic. These videos point to an interesting phenomenon of 'non-Chinese' speaking fluent Chinese and using their alignment with face masks to position themselves as 'prepared others' in contrast to the people around them. Rather than challenging the trope of 'the prepared' (the masked) vs 'the unprepared others' (the unmasked), these videos in some ways serve to reinforce the stereotype even more strongly. The enthusiastic speakers of Chinese who made these videos seem to want to position themselves as 'authentically Asian' by showcasing their affiliation with the culture of wearing face masks, which indexes 'Asian-ness'. The medium of video provides a space for language users to perform translanguaging. This translanguaging space allows social actors to occupy multiple positions through the creative use of semiotic resources, the editing of the video and other related affordances to constantly position and reposition themselves.

Whilst what is shown in the video can be considered a mundane activity (i.e. going to a supermarket), the video-creator draws on a wide range of multimodal

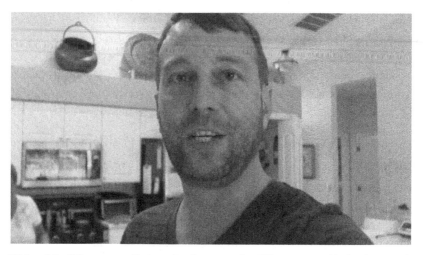

Video 4.1: [Live capture] America has over 1 million cases of infection. Let's go shopping with me and take a look at the real situation in the supermarket! (video embedded with permission from the video-creator, title of the video is translated by the author) (www.youtube.com/watch?v=Y9IS1OPslII)

and multilingual resources to connect it to more weighty issues of pandemic preparedness and cultural identity. Through these YouTube videos, these globalized, transnational video-creators use their rich linguistic and multi-modal repertoires to construct the position that wearing face masks is a matter of 'global citizenship'. These global participants are therefore important players in influencing the public's views about cultural practices of health.

Health Communication and Digital Technologies

In this section, I have shown how everyday, digitally mediated practices can be analysed using a framework informed by multimodality and translanguaging. Multimodality provides an analytical tool to systematically examine the multiplicity of modes in a particular instance of communication, and translanguaging allows us to appreciate how the video-creator draws on a repertoire of resources and breaks boundaries between the artificial divide separating the linguistic, paralinguistic and the extralinguistic. Through examining the orchestration of modes in a particular moment in the video, the video-creator's positioning is made visible.

As applied linguists, we are interested in how these new communicative practices play a role in the dissemination and construction of knowledge. As Blommaert (2020) observes, the COVID-19 outbreak accentuates the mobility of people and of knowledge. It remains to be seen how these creative, bottom-up vernacular practices of health communication, together with the advancement of technology, will continue to shape how we obtain information, and how certain beliefs are constructed throughout this crisis.

Acknowledgment

The author would like to thank Teacher Mike for giving us permission to embed his video in this section.

5 Investigating Media Representations of the Coronavirus in the UK, USA and Germany: What Can a Comparative Corpus-Based Discourse Analysis Contribute to Our Understanding of the COVID-19 Pandemic?

Sylvia Jaworska

Why a Comparative, Corpus-Based Discourse Analysis?

Through naming, describing and evaluating, media play a key role in creating representations of illness for public 'use'. Since many aspects of a disease – for example, a virus and its spread – are not visible to the naked eye and difficult to understand by non-experts, media reporting is for most people the prime source of health information; through the choice of language and images the media make the invisible visible influencing imaginaries, opinions and, in turn, responses to a health crisis (e.g. Dorfman & Wallack, 2007; Thibodeau & Boroditsky, 2011).

When, at the beginning of January 2020, many people from across the world were returning from the Christmas break while others were looking forward to celebrating the Chinese New Year, reports about a new and deadly virus started to circulate. Officially named SARS-CoV-2 and widely referred to as the coronavirus, the virus has since spread to most countries across the world leading to unprecedented health, social and economic consequences.

This small study explores some of the ways in which the coronavirus has been discursively constructed in the popular public media in three distinctive cultural and linguistic contexts: the UK, USA and Germany. Such comparisons are important for several reasons. With some exceptions (e.g. Antanasova & Koteyko, 2017), most discourse-analytical research on health and illness has focused mainly on one national context and one language. While such perspectives can offer rich insights into the representations of a discursive phenomenon, these representations are always 'bespoke' and restricted to that context and language, thus limiting our understating of how the phenomenon is 'seen' elsewhere (Leuschner & Jaworska, 2018; Partington et al., 2013). The coronavirus knows no borders and while the biological properties of the pathogen are everywhere the same, the ways in which the virus is talked about can be influenced by distinctive societal, cultural and linguistic factors. If we want to better understand the social reality of the COVID-19 pandemic, it is essential to compare how the virus has been represented in different contexts. Widely disseminated media outlets including national newspapers can offer some important insights into such representations. Moreover, comparisons across different contexts are important not only because they can limit some of the generalizations that are sometimes made (based on research on representations in English only) about the ways in which we talk about health and illness, but also for epistemo-logical reasons. Exploring how the coronavirus has been represented in public media discourse across different national contexts could uncover different ways of reasoning in relation to the pandemic and how they are reflected and reinforced through the language choices people make, potentially leading to a better under-standing of the pandemic and stimulating knowledge exchange.

This study examines media representations of the coronavirus by adopting the approach of a corpus-assisted discourse analysis (Baker, 2006; Partington et al., 2013). Corpus methods can be useful here for at least two reasons. First, a corpus approach gives us the opportunity to study collocations, that is, recurrent lexical choices occurring in the vicinity of the term under study. The concept of collocation goes back to the idea that the meanings of words are not just inherent in the prime word form but arise from the typical combin-ations of the word with other words in their context of use (Firth, 1957). The combination 'killer virus' can evoke different perceptions or associations than, for example, 'mortal virus'. Moreover, although in principle text pro-ducers have a larger pool of lexical items at their disposal, the choices that they make are likely to reflect deeper societal beliefs as well as ideological positions that in turn can reinforce particular kinds of representations and trigger particular outcomes (Stubbs, 2001). When the Trump administration has consistently referred to the coronavirus as the 'China virus', this choice serves, among other things, to blame the people of China for the spread of the disease, and led to a rise in prejudiced attitudes and stigmatization of Asians (The Editorial Board, 2020).

Secondly, a corpus-based approach relies on a quantitative investigation of large collections of texts based on automated frequency counts. This allows for lexical choices to be explored consistently across corpora. Findings obtained in this way can point to the existence of recurrent discursive patters and signal salient discourses around the studied phenomenon that an analysis of a few texts may not reveal (Baker, 2006); replicating the same procedures, we can then compare our findings systematically across corpora, shedding light on how the phenomenon in question is discursively constructed in different sources and languages (Partington et al., 2013; Jaworska & Leuschner, 2018).

Data and Methods

For the purpose of this study, three corpora of press coverage of the pandemic in the UK, USA and Germany were compiled using the database Nexis and two search terms 'coronavirus' and 'Covid-19'. Both terms were also used to extract data from German sources, since they have exact equivalents and are used so in

German. 7 January was selected as the starting point for the data collection because on that day the virus was officially confirmed to be a novel type of coronavirus. The end point was 31 March when the virus began to spread across the world leading to unprecedented lockdowns. Therefore, this study covers the initial outbreak of the COVID-19 pandemic.

Articles were collected from major national newspapers from the three countries that are available on Nexis. For the UK, the broadsheets *The Guardian*, *The Daily Telegraph* and *The Times* as well as 'regular' and middle-range tabloids such as *The Daily Mail*, *The Mirror* and *The Sun* were included. For the USA, *The New York Times*, *The New York Post*, *USA Today* and *Los Angeles Times* were included. The German corpus comprised articles from *Der Spiegel* (the most popular news magazine published weekly), *Die Tageszeitung (TAZ,)*, *Die Welt* and *Bunte* (a popular magazine similar in content and design to a tabloid). Table 5.1 shows the sizes of the three corpora. The differences reflect the availability of newspapers on Nexis and their status as daily or weekly newspapers or news magazines. For example, the two sources included in the DE-Corpus *Der Spiegel* and *Bunte* are weekly magazines and, hence, fewer articles are expected than in daily newspapers, which partially explains the smaller size of the German corpus.

To identify the dominant discursive construction of the coronavirus across the three national media contexts, collocations of the term 'coronavirus' were explored. The term was selected because at the time of the data collection, it was the most frequently used term in public discourse associated with the virus and the pandemic as evidenced in a study conducted by the team of the *Oxford English Dictionary* (OED, 2020); it has been more widely used than the official scientific term SARS-CoV-2, and the disease caused by the virus was not dubbed COVID-19 until early February 2020. To retrieve the collocations of 'coronavirus', the software programme Sketch Engine was used. In contrast to other similar programmes, Sketch Engine includes the tool Word Sketch, which specifies grammatical patterns of collocations allowing for the identification of, for example, the most salient verbal collocates depending on whether the search

Table 5.1 The sizes of the corpora

Corpus	No. of Articles	Corpus size
UK-Corpus	4,095	4,356,873
USA-Corpus	3,190	1,058,809
DE-Corpus	1,424	950,491

term is in the subject or object position (though errors occur in the classification and it is recommended to check the concordance lines to identify items that have been categorized inaccurately). Another benefit of using Sketch Engine is that it identifies collocates based on the Log Dice (LD) score, which is a measure of a collocation's salience and it does not depend on the total size of the corpus. This allows the researcher to have a consistent comparison measure across corpora of unequal sizes. Only collocations with a minimum frequency of 5 and LD score of 7 or above were considered, parameters also used in similar previous research.

Results

Table 5.2 shows the most salient collocations of 'coronavirus' in the UK press corpus. Only modifiers and verbs are included, since they emerged as the largest grammatical categories of all collocations identified. Striking is the use of many words from the domain of warfare or violence. Out of the fifty-one collocates shown in Table 5.1, twelve are specific references to military conflict ('battle', 'combat', 'surround', 'defeat', 'strike') or violence/physical fighting ('beat', 'fight', 'force', 'hit', 'tackle', 'strike'). These are shown in bold and seem to be particularly prominent (also in terms of raw frequencies) in the category of verbal collocates that occur with the search term as an object. This suggests that in this British press discourse measures of halting the pandemic were often framed as similar to those needed in a war or a fight.

A similar tendency, although with fewer instances of war references (eight in total), can be observed in the US press coverage (Table. 5.3). Here too, we find words such as 'fight', 'combat', 'kill', 'strike' and 'hit' in the vicinity of coronavirus suggesting a similar approach as in the UK press.

Looking at the German data (see Table 5.4), we find different items as salient collocations. Most striking is the absence of references to the militaristic language prominent in the two other corpora. Among the strongest verbal and modifying collocates of 'Coronavirus', only two verbs come from the domain of warfare 'bekämpfen' (to combat) and 'besiegen' (to defeat). But other words are much more salient and these include items that are, in turn, absent from the top collocates in the UK and US corpora. These include verbs such as 'testen' (to test) and 'schützen' (protect) as well as 'informieren' (inform), 'untersuchen' (investigate) and 'entwickeln' (develop) (the item 'test' is a noun collocate of 'coronavirus' in the UK-Corpus but is less salient than other collocates).

At the time of writing (July 2020), the pandemic situation in these three countries was different. In Germany, the spread of the virus seemed largely under control, while in the UK the infection rate was going down slowly and, in

Table 5.2 Collocations of 'coronavirus' in the UK-Corpus

Modifiers of 'coronavirus'			Verbs with 'coronavirus' as subject			Verbs with 'coronavirus' as object		
Modifier	Raw Freq.	LD Score	Verb	Raw Freq.	LD Score	Verb	Raw Freq.	LD Score
novel (noun)	115	11.51	cause	138	10.07	contract	184	11.04
new	435	10.92	affect	132	10.03	catch	83	10.05
novel (adjective)	49	10.28	spread	118	9.79	**fight**	66	9.77
deadly	44	9.91	**hit**	99	9.5	contain	80	9.73
suspected	23	9.01	pose	61	9.12	**tackle**	60	9.64
COVID-19	49	8.87	have	598	8.85	**combat**	51	9.5
terrible	10	8.08	reach	54	8.84	spread	57	9.48
fast-spreading	8	7.81	be	976	8.74	have	237	9.11
			continue	50	8.5	declare	33	8.63
			infect	38	8.45	treat	25	8.38
			die	37	8.01	get	47	8.32
			appear	29	7.88	regard	21	8.31
			impact	23	7.77	detect	18	8.08
			kill	22	7.64	confirm	42	7.91
			rise	28	7.61	**defeat**	15	7.9

force	20	7.54	**beat**	16	7.88
mean	21	7.47	call	21	7.86
become	22	7.35	surround	13	7.66
strike	17	7.34	transmit	12	7.55
do	28	7.15	discuss	13	7.48
			warn	15	7.48
			battle	11	7.46
			discover	11	7.44

Table 5.3 Collocations of 'coronavirus' in the US-Corpus

Modifiers of 'coronavirus'			Verbs with 'coronavirus' as subject			Verbs with 'coronavirus' as object		
Modifier	Raw Freq.	LD Score	Verb	Raw Freq.	LD Score	Verb	Raw Freq.	LD Score
novel (noun)	226	12.54	cause	171	11.23	contract	82	10.89
new	458	11.75	spread	106	10.49	spread	63	10.54
novel (adjective)	59	10.79	continue	52	9.44	**fight**	40	9.92
deadly	42	10.06	affect	45	9.42	contain	38	9.7
current	8	7.51	**hit**	37	9.1	catch	30	9.6
			infect	29	8.9	**combat**	23	9.28
			pose	28	8.86	have	133	8.96
			have	271	8.84	prevent	22	8.35
			be	455	8.57	treat	19	8.77
			appear	21	8.24	get	40	8.59
			become	21	8.07	**battle**	11	8.31
			break	15	7.95	declare	13	8.24
			grow	16	7.94	transmit	9	8.02
			strike	13	7.78	**beat**	8	7.81
			kill	13	7.72	address	9	7.79

disrupt	10	7.42	handle	8	7.67
threaten	10	7.4	believe	8	7.64
make	15	7.38	confront	7	7.63
emerge	10	7.35	call	11	7.58
begin	13	7.28	know	10	7.53
turn	10	7.28	stop	8	7.49
force	9	7.23	dismiss	6	7.49
go	15	7.19	regard	6	7.42
			discuss	6	7.34
			cure	5	7.23
			regard	6	7.42
			think	8	7.41
			limit	7	7.22
			surround	5	7.15

Table 5.4 Collocations of 'Coronavirus' in the DE-Corpus

Modifiers of 'coronavirus'			Verbs with 'coronavirus' as subject			Verbs with 'coronavirus' as an accusative object			Verbs with 'coronavirus' as a dative object		
Modifier	Raw Freq.	LD Score	Verb	Raw Freq.	LD Score	Verb	Raw Freq.	LD Score	Modifier	Raw Freq.	LD Score
neuartig	182	12.94	ausbreiten	13	10.53	testen	35	11.37	infizieren	42	12.05
neu	114	10.98	verbreiten	8	9.78	eindämmen	7	9.25	anstecken	19	11.15
positiv	16	9.65	wüten	6	9.62	entwickeln	6	8.87	schützen	11	10.4
ausbreitend	9	9.26	sorgen	6	9.31	**bekämpfen**	4	8.65	sterben	6	9.3
grassierend	5	8.38	treffen	7	9.15	treffen	6	8.55	verhindern	5	8.79
aktuell	8	8.13	legen	6	9.15	stehen	6	8.48	erkranken	6	8.76
gefährlich	5	7.8	grassieren	5	9.04	**besiegen**	5	8.38	umgehen	5	8.66
rund	7	7.68	spielen	6	8.83	vergleichen	6	8.34			
kurz	5	7.47	bedeuten	5	8.82	untersuchen	5	8.27			
			greifen	5	8.69	informieren	6	8.08			
						nutzen	5	7.83			

the USA, it was still rising. This has to do, in part, with the different national responses to the pandemic. Germany was relatively quick in introducing a lockdown and widespread testing, and hence it should not be surprising to see 'testen' (to test) as one of the top verbal collocates. The prominence of 'untersuchen' (investigate) and 'entwicklen' (develop) points further to an approach grounded in science, while 'schützen' (protect) places an emphasis on a care and protection. The UK reacted more slowly to the pandemic and had a limited testing capacity. Its response was characterized by an invocation of the 'Blitz spirit' of WWII. Examples of the war language around the pandemic from the UK-Corpus include headlines such as:

1 Why our <u>hero</u> health staff are no1 <u>defence</u> against covid-19 (*The Sun*)
2 NHS and private hospitals join <u>forces</u> to <u>fight</u> coronavirus (*The Guardian*)
3 We are at <u>war</u> against the virus (*Daily Mail*)

The fewer instances of war and violence metaphors in the US-Corpus may also be a reflection of the pandemic timeline and the rather inactive stance on the part of its government during the initial outbreak. The conspicuous absence of war and violence metaphors in the DE-Corpus may have historical reasons; war rhetoric and specifically words coined during the Nazi period are not common as source domains in the German press discourse and are used predominatly in original historical references (Schröter, 2018).[2]

The use of war metaphors in the context of a pandemic is problematic. They can sometimes be constructive in that they can mobilize public health efforts. Yet, when it comes to patients, particularly those who suffer from deadly conditions, they can be distressing, and even unethical, especially if the patients or their doctors are not 'winning the battle' (e.g. Semino et al., 2018; Sontag, 1989). Also, the kind of qualities that a military mobilization requires, such as strong character and physical strength are, in and of themselves, not going to weaken the virulence of the pathogen which spreads quickly through close human contact. The virus does not distinguish between 'friends' and 'enemies'; it can affect us all, whatever our physical strength and moral stance. As we have seen, testing and prevention measures as well as clear public communication are more successful.

---

[2] There seems to be a high degree of sensitivity in Germany when it comes to the use of language around the pandemic; in a recent debate streamed on the acclaimed Coronavirus-Update Podcast (produced by NDR – Norddeutscher Rundfunk 'Northern German Broadcast'), which includes prominent scientists and social scientists, the use of the word 'Bewältigung' (overcoming) in the context of dealing with the Corona crisis was criticised as inappropriate because it is strongly associated with the 'Vergangenheitsbewältigung' (overcoming the past), where the past means the Nazi past (see www.ndr.de/nachrichten/info/podcast4685.html).

Conclusion

The study illustrates the usefulness of studying collocations to uncover dominant ways of representing the coronavirus; it demonstrates how they can shed light on discourses that are salient but not necessarily obvious to the researcher. Metaphors were not a specific focus of this study; yet they have emerged as an important linguistic device in the discourses around 'coronavirus' in the UK and US corpora. This study has also shown the benefits of a comparative approach clearly indicating that what can be said about the pandemic and how it can be said depends on the linguistic and cultural factors including different local histories. The relative absence of war metaphors in the German public discourse around 'coronavirus' is a single but compelling case in point. Since the national media are, for most people, the first source of health information, studying how the media report on the novel virus is critical if we want to understand public responses to the pandemic. The way in which the media choose words to frame the virus may itself lead the population to respond in more or less effective ways. Yet, this study is small in scope and does not utilize the full potential of corpus-based methods to study discourse (see Baker, 2006; Partington et al., 2013). It has considered collocations only and as de-contextualized items presented in lists; further research is needed to explore how they were used in the press discourse investigated here, taking into consideration a wider range of lexico-grammatical properties of the studied languages including, for example, the genitive objects in German and noun collocations in both English and German.

6 Sense and Sensibility: Urban Public Signs during a Pandemic

Zhu Hua

In this section, I will examine the linguistic landscape in an ordinary high street in North West London during the early days of the COVID-19 pandemic lockdown when many retail businesses were told to close overnight. I will demonstrate how shops responded to the crisis, how words and images communicate their authors' sense and sensibility towards the crisis, and what we can learn from this kind of unprecedented '*in vivo*' crisis communication.

Originating in the field of language planning around the 1990s, linguistic landscape (LL) studies are primarily concerned with language and images in public spaces (Shohamy & Gorter, 2009). Their aim, according to the *Linguistic Landscape* journal, is 'to understand the motives, uses, ideologies, language varieties and contestations of multiple forms of "languages" as they are displayed in public spaces.' Many LL studies used quantitative or comparative methods in which signs in a certain area were systematically photographed and the different languages used on different types of signs, (e.g. official vs non-official signs, public vs private signs) were compared to indicate the relative power and vitality of linguistic communities (e.g. Backhaus, 2006; Ben-Rafael et al., 2006; Cenoz & Gorter, 2006). In the last decade, LL studies have expanded their conceptualizations, methodologies and applications (for a review, see Lou, 2016; Shohamy & Gorter, 2009). Particularly relevant to the theme of this volume, the conceptual incorporation of multimodal and social semiotic theories has enabled LL studies to go beyond texts and to offer a means of bridging different modalities and approaching semiotic resources as a whole. Methodologically, LL studies have become integrated into or combined with ethnography, whereby the meanings of words are closely examined in the contexts where they appear and nuanced insights are offered about the relationship between language, society and people. In terms of applications, LL studies have been applied to education, learning and political activism. While a small number of studies have examined linguistic landscapes during conflict and protests (e.g. Mamadouh, 2018), very few have investigated the impact of crisis on linguistic landscapes (cf. Gogonas & Maligkoudi, 2019). The study presented in this section aims to contribute to the emerging debates on urban public signs in times of crisis.

Data Collection: When and Where

The UK government imposed lockdown measures in England on 26 March 2020. People were directed to stay home except for essential travel for work, grocery shopping, medical needs and caring duties as well as one form of exercise per day. Many retail businesses which were deemed non-essential were closed overnight and no one knew at that time that this closure would last for three months and more. It was not until 4 July when most of the shops were allowed to reopen with strict social distancing measures. Walking down empty streets during my daily walks, I could not help noticing the new signs in shop fronts and other public spaces. I started collecting the images of shop signs on Golders Green Road, London. While there was limited access to sign authors or owners, this kind of walking ethnography on familiar territories turned out to be a convenient, but meaningful, means of data collection regarding changes in the linguistic landscape during the crisis, adding insights to the conversation on 'ethnographic fieldwork quarantined' (e.g. Kuiper, 2020).

The street is popular with local residents and visitors who have connections with the area. It functions as a community hub, with a local library branch, a Greek orthodox church, several synagogues and Jewish community learning centres. While the area is known for being a 'Jewish' area, it is very mixed with other communities such as Japanese, Korean, Indian and Black African, according to the 2011 census data (www.streetcheck.co.uk/postcodedistrict/nw11; and https://hid den-london.com/gazetteer/golders-green/). This multicultural character is also reflected in the presence of a number of 'ethnic' shops and restaurants and reinforced by the presence of multilingual signages in a variety of languages (some shop-front images are available through the Google Map and other online collections of photo images such as alamy.com). Along with KFC, Costa cafe, high street banks, etc., there are Polish, Korean and Turkish shops, Chinese medicine clinics, sushi restaurants, as well as a Greek hairdresser, a Romanian shop, among others. A major Golders Green Town Centre Strategy, which provides detailed guidance on shop-front design and decoration, was developed by the Barnet Council to accommodate growth and investment in 2019 (https://engage .barnet.gov.uk/golders-green-town-centre-strategy) and it is unclear at the time of writing this section what the Council's decision is and how the pandemic is going to impact its implementation, if approved.

The analysis reported in this section is based on about 200 signs observed and photographed along the Golders Green Road between the period of 26 March and 4 June 2020. The changes in three areas (i.e. media of writing, content and language choices) are most noticeable to me as a resident living in the area for more than a decade. The main findings were originally published as a blog piece on the viral discourse website (https://viraldiscourse.com/) on 7 June 2020. I plan to continue to collect the signs during the phrase of the lockdown easing and the 'new normal'.

Handwriting

The first thing I noticed while photographing the shop signs and observing changes in shop fronts was the abrupt appearance of handwritten signs on shop windows and doors in the first few weeks of the lockdown. In my recent research on handwritten signs in public spaces (Li & Zhu, 2020), we have discussed how the medium of handwriting indexes spontaneity and informality as well as the identity and personality of writers. Here we see how these handwritten signs additionally convey, and contribute to, the sense of emergency and are used to communicate affect and to connect people. Clearly, they were written and put up quickly, but with a considerable amount of concern for the readers/customers.

In Figure 6.1, a handwritten sign is sellotaped to the door of a restaurant, with all the letters in capitals and the word 'CLOSED' underlined. Notwithstanding the small grammar mistake, the brief sign re-semiotizes the government's instructions, attributing the closure to COVID-19 and putting things on hold 'until further notice'. Its brevity and matter of fact style, while appearing to be calm, speaks of a sense of helplessness.

In another handwritten sign (Fig. 6.2), the message focuses on customer relations. It is styled as an open letter to friends in a poetic form. The sign consists of two key messages written over two pieces of paper placed together. The top half is a thank you message with "YOU" in quotation marks – a possible explanation for the emphasis is to mark that this is not

Figure 6.1 'Due Covid-19, closed until further notice'

Figure 6.2 'Thank "you" We dont know when But we will see you "again"'

just an ordinary occasion when we say thank you as a matter of routine. It is said with emphasis, sincerity and thoughtfulness. The second half is a promise carefully choreographed into four lines: 'we do not know when but we will see you again'. The key words 'when' and 'again' are highlighted with spaces or quotation marks. This half, while appearing to address the factual question of when the shop will reopen, is an ingenious recontextualization. It reminds us of 'We'll Meet Again', a 1939 British song made famous by Vera Lynn. The very lyrics were used by Queen Elizabeth to urge the British people to stay strong when she addressed the nation soon after the lockdown in March.

Elsewhere, in a picture taken and tweeted by Caroline Eden (who has kindly given me permission to use the photo here), we see an extraordinary example of how handwritten signs can become a dialogue between people who may be otherwise unrelated and thereby create the space to communicate mutual care with a good sense of humour. In Figure 6.3, below the handwritten sign of 'closed I'm afraid' on the window is a handwritten response from a keen customer or a passer-by. In the long note, the person positions themselves as a careful, perhaps a bit pedantic, reader, and plays with the ambiguity of the shop's message. In offering two possible interpretations of the speech acts conveyed in the original message, the response focuses on the effect of the

Figure 6.3 'Closed I'm afraid' (photograph by Caroline Eden taken in Stockbridge, Edinburgh, on 18 June)

speech act has on listeners, or in Austin's (1975) term, perlocutionary act. Thus, a transactional act becomes an interpersonal act.

Dear owner,
Thank you for your lovely message related to your current trading status. Unfortunately, due to limited punctuation we are unsure about your meaning.

Do you mean "Closed, I'm afraid"? In which case we thank you for your polite recognition of the inconvenience caused to us, your customers, of such closure.

Or, do you mean 'Closed. I'm afraid.' In which case our hearts go out to you at this, indeed, worrying time. Thanks for sharing. It is important to recognise our own mental state and be open with others.

#stay safe.

Directives vs Pleas

Some of the shops which managed to remain open customized their shop signs in relation to the risk and demand depending on the remit of their business. We see a new kind of customer relationship in these signages. For those 'less essential' shops, many used specially designed signs to communicate and mark the fact that they were still in operation. These signs tended to be more professional looking with a touch of design. I found several of these signs on mobile notice boards placed on pavements, presumably to attract customers' attention. Both the signs included here are printed rather than handwritten with the wording 'open', the most important communicative content, displayed in the most visible way. In Figure 6.4, the sentence appears as a headline and uses large fonts and clear contrastive colours. In Figure 6.5, each word is in full capitals and arranged as a single line. The texts are carefully worded too. The presence of the adverbial phrases of time, '*still*' and '*as usual*', emphasize that the shops continue to operate, contrary to what may have been expected. The main business of the shops (vitamin and supplement shops in the former case and a postal delivery service in the latter) did not appear on top of the list of shops allowed to remain open by the government and these businesses clearly felt the need to go out of their way to make a plea to potential customers. So these signs serve as the perfect means of informing and advertising, two elements in Scollon and Scollon's (2003) taxonomy of the functions of public signs.

For those shops offering essential services such as pharmacies, banks and supermarkets, signs are used as directives, (safe)guarding the space within. Here are the shop fronts of three pharmacies on the high street in my neighbourhood. 'Do not enter' signs (Fig. 6.6), deterring unwanted customers who have any COVID-19 symptoms, are clearly visible in the picture of the first

Figure 6.4 We are still open

Figure 6.5 Open as usual

Figure 6.6 'Do not enter ... '

pharmacy. It is red and includes the logo of the 'NHS' at the bottom. In fact, the logo of the 'NHS' occurs in many of the signs found on the pharmacy facades. Its presence gives the deterrent signs a kind of authority. The second pharmacy is a Boots branch (Fig. 6.7). Its shop front is almost excessively busy with posters with information and signs about handwashing and social distancing. The third one has fewer posters (Fig. 6.8). There are two signs declaring: 'Do not enter' (one in red and the other in black) on each side of glass doors. There is also a sign declaring zero tolerance for abuse of staff. While the pharmacies vary in the extent of signage used, all the signs are printed rather than handwritten and carry a sense of top-down directives. These businesses almost seem keen to direct customers away, rather than welcome them in, an unusual customer relationship in a time of crisis.

Multilingual Signage

The implementation of social distancing in shops means that each shop has to decide how many people they can allow in. And interestingly, this seems to attract

Figure 6.7 A Boots branch

Figure 6.8 A pharmacy

signs in languages other than English. The Polish bakery and Polish grocery shop, which are close to each other, use bilingual signs with English first and Polish second (Figs. 6.9 and 6.10). The same wording suggests that one of them may have copied the other, although one has a minor typo in English. The English sign on the two-metre social distancing rule might have been made by the shop owners themselves. The wording (when possible, maintain at least a 2 metre (6 feet) distance from others) is more of a plea than a directive. It contains a lesser degree of obligation than the government's official line. The third one uses Romanian only (Fig. 6.11). It says 'maximum 2 people are allowed in the store at the same time'. The presence of multilingual signs of crisis communication is rare on the whole. Many ethnic shops in the area use English only.

Discussion and Conclusion

Crisis impacts linguistic landscape and at the same time, linguistic landscape feeds into the sense of crisis. The media of signs matters. As we have seen in this analysis, shops and retailers developed ways of communicating their sense and sensibilities towards crisis and risk spontaneously in the earlier days of the lockdown. The sudden and prominant appearance of handwritten signs, along with how and where they are posted, becomes a significant part of the semiotic landscape of crisis. It is not surprising to see handwriting, with its spontaneity

Figure 6.9 A Polish Bakery

Figure 6.10 A Polish grocery shop

Figure 6.11 A Romanian shop

and accessibility, become a convenient medium during crisis. After all, this was an emergency situation and printed signs might not be readily accessible. What is new, however, is that the handwritten signs create space for sensibility. They are silent messengers that remind the passers-by that we are in a different, extraordinary time and space. They tell the stories of their authors – how they respond to the crisis, how they feel, and how they see the future when so much is up in the air. They constitute a kind of *in vivo* crisis communication we have not seen before in the study of urban public signs.

The importance of media is further demonstrated through the contrast between the sense and sensibility conveyed through handwriting and directives and warning displayed in print signage that regulates visitors' or shoppers' behaviours. The new customer relationship under social distancing rules is a delicate one – it needs to carefully balance business interests, (multilingual) customer needs, health risks and government guidelines available only in English at the time. Despite the significant presence of multicultural population in the area, few shops resort to multilingual signages to communicate crisis and to guide their customers about social distancing rules.

The lack of multilingual signs is particularly concerning as it reflects a wider picture of multilingualism in crisis. LL studies provide insights into the relative power of languages in a society and, in particular, the exclusive and inclusive effect of the use of languages other than English in signs in public spaces. What we have seen during the present crisis in the UK is the predominance of English over other languages (this observation is echoed in the blogs by Grey, 2020 and Hopkyns, 2020). The function of other languages is mostly reduced to minimal information-giving, as we have seen in the bilingual examples in the aforementioned analysis. At the same time, the information from the UK government website (gov.uk) and the NHS website about COVID-19 were all in English as of early July 2020. The lack of public information in other languages is a particular concern when so much depends on the public understanding and complying with the rules and the regulations. What does the new vocabulary, with words such as 'lockdown', 'social distancing', 'self-isolation' and 'face covering' (which is not equivalent to 'face mask') – terms that were not part of our daily conversation before the pandemic but which now we can now say in one breath – mean in other cultures and other languages? And how do the people who speak other languages figure out the degree of obligation in the government's key messages and directives? What does 'exceptional circumstances' mean when there have been so many debates about social distancing rules recently, debates that have taken place almost entirely in English? Has this lack of information partly contributed to the high death toll among BAME (Black, Asian and Minority Ethnic) communities in the UK? Amid the pandemic, we see the vulnerability of multilingualism and its speakers. We see multilingualism itself in crisis.

7 When the Internet Gets 'Coronafied': Pandemic Creativity and Humour in Internet Memes

Erhan Aslan

After its first outbreak in late 2019 in Wuhan, China, the COVID-19 pandemic became a global health crisis of unprecedented magnitude in a very short time span. The pandemic forced billions of people around the world to stay home in quarantines and lockdowns and quickly adapt to sudden changes in living and working conditions. Along with the increase in digital communication during this time, a massive number of jokes, puns, Tweets, TikTok videos and internet memes about coronavirus began to spread on various social media platforms.

Of these various digital artefacts of the pandemic, this section focuses on internet memes. Even though internet memes are a relatively new genre in digital discourse, the concept of memes existed long before the digital era. The term meme is rooted in evolutionary biology, coined by Richard Dawkins (1976) in his famous book *The Selfish Gene*. The word comes from the Greek *mimema*, meaning 'imitated' which Dawkins shortened to rhyme with gene. Memes indeed resemble genes in the sense that the transmission of cultural units is like the transmission of genes. During the transmission process, memes undergo changes by means of copying and imitation. Traditional examples of cultural memes are bird songs, rumours, catchphrases, stories, fashion, etc. The cultural units or memes of a society reflect deep social and cultural structures and can reveal the hidden ideologies rooted within them.

Defined by Shifman (2014: 14) as 'a group of digital items sharing common characteristics of content, form, and/or stance, which were created with awareness of each other, and were circulated, imitated, and/or transformed via the internet by many users, internet memes can take numerous forms, such as videos or photoshopped images. In order for an internet meme to emerge and spread, there first needs to be a viral event or phenomenon that will encourage internet users to engage in various forms of derivative work. News, sensationalistic media moments, or a music video can spread to the masses via digital word-of-mouth mechanisms through likes and shares without significant change. Once the event or phenomenon has gone viral and reached a large number of people, certain features of this event will encourage extensive creative user engagement in several derivative forms (see Vasquez & Aslan, 2020). One of the most commonly used form of internet memes on social media platforms is the image macro. Dynel (2016: 663) defines the image macro as 'a captioned image that typically consists of a picture and a witty message or a catchphrase'. A political controversy, natural disaster, celebrity scandal or some internet phenomenon can easily lead to the quick birth, proliferation and spread of internet memes as a digital public response mechanism. Internet memes not only constitute creative responses to online viral content or an emerging social crisis, but also allow us to collectively process current issues, events and people. They mirror real-life behaviours, experiences and stances in uniquely humorous ways. They also allow people to connect with each other and create a sense of community and levity. Research on humour and internet memes is growing, as evidenced by recent publications from disciplines such as anthropology (Haynes, 2019), communication, journalism and new media (Miltner, 2014; Penney, 2019; Taecharungroj & Nueangjamnong, 2015) and linguistics (Dynel, 2016; Piata, 2016). In order to contribute to this body of research, in this section I present a preliminary analysis of a set of COVID-19 internet memes from a multimodal digital discourse analysis perspective.

The focus of this section is on the spread of COVID-19 on a global scale affecting millions of people and the emergence of humorous internet memes generated and shared by internet users. Most internet memes about COVID-19 have been innocently humorous, focusing on daily hygiene practices such as handwashing, face masks, toilet paper, home quarantines, videoconferences and the challenges of working from home. The goal of this section is to explore how internet users use different linguistic and semiotic resources creatively to express humour especially during the early phases of the pandemic.

Data and Method

In order to create a corpus of image macro memes related to COVID-19, I began collecting data from multiple online platforms in March 2020. The main data source was Facebook which I used to identify widely shared image macros as they appeared in the newsfeed of my personal account through shares by my friends and acquaintances. I also searched for memes on a major meme database (http://knowyourmeme.com/) with specific keywords such as 'coronavirus', 'Covid-19' 'lockdown' 'quarantine' 'self-isolation', 'handwashing' 'toilet paper' 'social distancing' 'working from home' and examined other relevant themes and entries that were added to the database (e.g. quarantine memes, celebrity hand sanitizer comparisons, Miss Rona, etc.). Additionally, I did a similar keyword search on Google images, which helped me identify other relevant image macros. What I present in this section is primarily representative of the early stages of COVID-19 lockdown that began towards the end of March 2020 in many countries. I published an earlier draft of this report in late April 2020 on the Viral Discourse blog.

In this section, I draw on principles from multimodal digital discourse analysis to explore the multimodal humour in image macro memes. Multimodal discourse analysis has focused heavily on discourses that appear in digital communication because of the rich combination of text, picture, audio and video that digital media make possible. Image macros are defined as 'text-image multimodal discourse made up of one or two text lines at the top and/or the bottom of the meme complemented by an image in the middle with several possible interpretive combinations' (Yus, 2020: 5). According to Jewitt (2016), one assumption in multimodal analysis is that modes occur together in every instance of communication, have specialized roles, and that these roles and the relationships between modes are essential to meaning making. Due to the multimodal nature of internet memes, the grammatical composition of memetic texts cannot solely depend on linguistic forms or visual means (Milner, 2016), and decoding the eventual meaning of memes is not possible through obtaining the partial meanings of text or picture taken separately, but only from their combined meanings (Yus, 2019).

Language is not merely used to communicate, but it often serves as a means for self-expression and amusement. Humans generally use language in ways that deviate from expected and regular compositional features of language for creative purposes. Creative use of language often involves some attention to form and with the express purpose of bonding with others by playing with language form. In a similar vein, memetic humour relies heavily on creative multimodality, meaning that it involves the combination of creative texts, images, hyperlinks and other visual features. Creative multimodality can be achieved by various linguistic mechanisms. In what follows, I will present an analysis of three elements of humour in COVID-19 internet memes, namely *intertextuality*, *wordplay*, and *incongruity*.

Intertextuality

In memetic communication, internet users tend to draw on previously known cultural texts and make cross references to different popular culture events, icons or phenomena. Memetic humour relies heavily on the combination of familiar and well-known knowledge and references with current situations and experiences in unique, creative and surprising ways. This creative blending is called intertextuality. Intertextuality can occur on a textual and visual level. In Figure 7.1 (skywalk3r, 2020), COVID-19 is linked to the popular dance drama film *Saturday Night Fever* starring John Travolta and the film's soundtrack *Stayin' Alive* (by The Bee Gees). This example shows two layers of intertextuality. One layer involves the word 'fever' in the film title as referring to one of

BREAKING NEWS ...

John Travolta was hospitalized for suspected COVID-19, but doctors now confirm that it was only Saturday Night Fever, and they assure everyone that he is Staying Alive.

Figure 7.1 Staying Alive

the common symptoms of COVID-19. The other layer involves a connection between the soundtrack title 'staying alive' and surviving COVID-19. Additionally, the meme is presented in the format of breaking news and the presence of John Travolta's quizzical and amused look in the image strengthens the source connection (i.e. cultural referent) as well as the humorous meaning that he is alive and healthy.

Other examples of intertextuality highlighting other aspects of COVID-19 include the meme *All of a sudden, everyone has become Sheldon* (u/rastafaryn, 2020) in Figure 7.2, featuring the hygiene freak character Sheldon from the popular TV show *The Big Bang Theory* spraying disinfectant into the air and covering his mouth; another is an image (The Shining Memes 2020) from the film *The Shining* highlighting isolation with family (Fig. 7.3); and the arm cutting scene from *Terminator 2* featured in another meme, *Me after washing my hands for 20 seconds for 57 times a day* (godoftitsandmemes, 2020) (Fig. 7.4).

Wordplay

Wordplay is a productive source of humour in internet memes that involves the clever and witty use of words at the textual level. Wordplay techniques use multiple meanings and the similar sounds of words to create humorous effects. Some of the COVID-19 vocabulary that entered into our daily use of language has been subject to wordplay. One particular word, for example, is *quarantine*:

In Figures 7.5 (makeameme.org, 2020a) and 7.6 (makeameme.org, 2020b), we see a creative play on the *–tine* part of the word (quaran+tine) which results

Figure 7.2 All of a sudden everybody has become Sheldon

Figure 7.3 Isolation with family

in new words and meanings *quaran+tini* – a martini to drink alone at home and *quaran+teen* – the current teen generation experiencing home quarantines and lockdowns. Another creative blend that we see in other memes for the hypothetical new generation of children conceived during COVID-19 as a result of people being quarantined at home is *coronials*, resulting from a play on

Me after washing my hands for 20
seconds 57 times in one day

Figure 7.4 Me after washing my hands for 20 seconds for 57 times a day

Figure 7.5 Quarantini

coronavirus and *millennials* (Fig. 7.7, makeameme.org, 2020c). In these examples, while we see a creative mechanism in the textual component of the memes, the visual components play a complementary role in interpreting the humorous meanings conveyed. For example, in Figure 7.5, the image of an actual martini enables us to associate the new word *quarantini* with a martini, and without this image, this association may not be easily accessible to viewers. Similarly, in Figure 7.6, the angry face of a teenage girl conveys the

Figure 7.6 Quaran-teen

psychological state of mind of teenagers during COVID-19 as a result of not being able to go to school and due to the cancellations of major events like prom, graduation and other social activities. In Figure 7.7, the image of a newborn unit is crucial in interpreting the word coronial as a new generation of babies born during COVID-19.

Figure 7.7 Coronials

Spelling is another wordplay technique that can lead to humorous creative blends. One example is the misspelling of the word *quarantine* as *cornteen*. Some argue that it may have originated from an actual misspelling of quarantine but it may also be used deliberately to joke about how the word might be pronounced in different regional dialects. In Figure 7.8, we see a meme blend using the popular rap singer Drake's image from his 2015 hit single *Hotline Bling*. According to knowyourmeme.com, the original image is typically used in memes to express one's disdain of some topic or something said by another person. In the first image right next to the word *cornteen* in Figure 7.8 (imgflip. com, 2020a), we see Drake holding his hand up to the side of his face while looking disgusted, while in the second image at the bottom, his content look indicates his approval of the spelling of the word as *quarantine* that appears right next to the bottom image.

There have also been several puns on the word *corona*. The coronavirus is named after the Latin word for crown due to its exterior structure that features small crown-like spikes. The word corona is also the name of a Mexican beer that is named after the Sun's corona. Corona being both a virus and a beer name has led to some humorous uptake by internet users. In Figure 7.9 (imglip.com, 2020b) is an example of this association. In the bottom text there is another playful use of the word lime referring to Lyme disease. The visual referents here (i.e. the beer bottle and the lime wedge) are crucial in interpreting the humour.

Coronavirus is sometimes shortened to *corona*, which is further shortened to *rona*. According to Dictionary.com, *Rona* – often in the phrase *the rona* – is a reduced form of *coronavirus* and has become a playful or ironic way

Figure 7.8 Cornteen

Figure 7.9 Corona virus

to refer to COVID-19, especially when commenting on more relatable, humorous challenges of social distancing during the pandemic. There are examples of coronavirus being personified with the name *rona*, as can be seen in Figure 7.10 (secretNinja, 2020) where a concerned dog image accompanies two levels of text, the top one indicating a possible symptom of COVID-19 (tickle in throat) and the bottom one is the personified coronavirus:

Another creative blend is *COVID-19* and *idiot, covidiot,* a slang insult for someone who disregards health and safety guidelines associated with the coronavirus. Figure 7.11 (makeameme.org, 2020d) is a meme blend utilizing the template of another meme (Grandma finds the internet) featuring an elderly woman looking at a laptop computer screen with captions expressing shock and bewilderment at what she discovers online. In this example, the image of the shocked grandma is juxtaposed with her learning about the word covidiot. *Moronavirus*, a similar blend derived from the words *moron* and *coronavirus*, is another quarantine shaming word. The US President Donald Trump is depicted as 'moronavirus' by plavonk (2020) in Figure 7.12, in which his angry-looking face is plastered onto a virus image:

Incongruity

Internet memes frequently involve unexpected combinations of two or more elements, known as incongruity. Such juxtapositions significantly contribute to a meme's success. Suls (1972) contends that incongruous elements

Figure 7.10 Rona

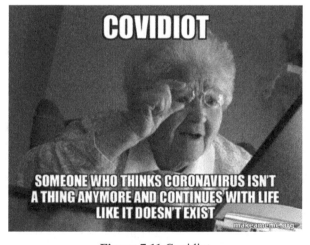

Figure 7.11 Covidiot

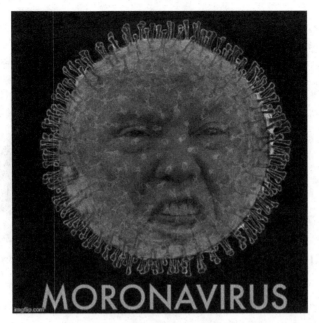

Figure 7.12 Trump virus

convey humorous meanings if the recipient knows that a particular stimulus is a joke. Therefore, it is not sufficient to have two incongruous elements to appear together but a humorous intent underlying a joke needs to be recognized. In Figure 7.13 (Bosh, 2020), a marine biologist working from home is featured. There are several opposing elements being creatively juxtaposed here which results in humour. One element is the context opposition – a marine biologist working in a bathtub vs in the ocean. The incongruity is intensified in the visual component of the meme, particularly the image showing a man wearing diving equipment in the bathtub. The textual part of the meme highlights and parodies working from home due to the social isolation requirements (given that doing fieldwork in the ocean would not be possible for a marine biologist at home).

Conclusion

In this section, I presented a preliminary analysis of COVID-19 memes by focusing on image macro memes. The initial findings show that the multimodal structure of internet memes allows users to exploit both visual and textual strategies to create humorous meanings by drawing on various multimodal and linguistic mechanisms such as intertextuality, wordplay and juxtaposition of incongruous elements.

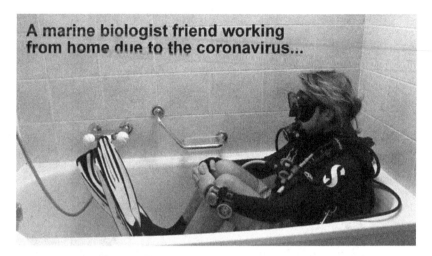

Figure 7.13 A marine biologist friend working from home due to coronavirus

What I aimed to do in this section is to provide a glimpse of how internet memes as digital artefacts of online communication can shed light on ordinary people's perceptions and experiences during an unprecedented global pandemic. Owing to their multimodal nature, internet memes provide new resources for internet users to create humorous messages by exploiting various linguistic and semiotic mechanisms, as shown in the examples. The humour and creativity in online communication at a time of global pandemic appears to be a helpful resource for people in coping with the psychological impacts of this pandemic. The myriad memes on the internet show us that memetic humour is not just a coping mechanism in times of mass tragedy and uncertainty but at the same time a creative mechanism to engage with some complex social and political issues provoked by crisis situations. In this vein, internet memes can be considered an ideal medium to express and hear multiple voices, identities and opinions of ordinary people through shared cultural and political references and create a common view. Although memes can be easily dismissed as trivial in terms of their content, Milner (2016: 14) explains that these 'small expressions' actually have 'big implications'. In other words, memes extend to larger cultures or audiences and often make connections between feelings and values, positions or beliefs, potentially shedding light on social structures and related ideologies and discourses.

8 #HateIsAVirus: Talking about COVID-19 'Hate'
Carmen Lee

An April 2020 report published by moonshot (2020) found that there had been a 300 per cent rise in hashtags on Twitter that 'encourage or incite violence against China and Chinese people'. Anti-Chinese hate speech spiked after US President Donald Trump first referred to the coronavirus as the 'China Virus' and 'Chinese Virus' in March 2020. But just exactly how does a name become 'hate'? Can a name alone incite racism and violence?

This section explores how concepts of critical discourse analysis (CDA) can inform our understanding of COVID-19 'hate' as a discursive action. It aims to problematize existing definitions of hate speech and how its meaning is discursively constructed and reappropriated by social actors. CDA is particularly relevant to understanding the discourse of and about hate speech because it is such discourse that shapes people's ideas and attitudes, and eventually, their decisions to behave aggressively or not online. A critical discourse-analytic approach enables researchers to uncover how potentially harmful discourse is often legitimized and justified, and how these strategies are linguistically realized. For an overview of CDA principles and their application, see Wodak (2015).

In CDA, both microlinguistic devices and macro-discourse strategies are considered. An initial observation of a small set of posts and comments from Twitter collected between March and May 2020 reveals some recurring linguistic and discourse strategies of COVID-19 hate speech, from explicit forms of verbal aggression, such as expletives, to implicit discourse strategies or 'soft hate speech' (Assimakopoulos, 2020) such as dehumanizing metaphors (e.g. calling mainland Chinese people 蝗蟲 *locusts*) and personification. For example, in a reply to a Twitter comment written in simplified Chinese, someone calls the characters 殘體字 (*handicapped writing*). The simplified Chinese writing system is the official character writing system in mainland China that is characterized by fewer strokes per character, compared to the traditional character writing system adopted in Hong Kong and Taiwan. Personifying a writing system as handicapped or disabled allows the commenter to negatively evaluate out-groups or anyone who uses that writing system as insufficient. This enables speakers or writers to construct an us–them dichotomy, a common discourse strategy in racist discourse (Reisigl & Wodak, 2005).

Discourse is historically situated. When we situate COVID-related hate in the history of verbal aggression, online or offline, it is nothing new. Expressions such as 'locusts' and 'handicapped writing' were already prevalent before COVID-19. The debate over simplified Chinese characters has intensified over the years, especially in Hong Kong, where traditional writing is still used. As political tensions between Hong Kong and mainland China have surged, these terms have also become prevalent in anti-Chinese discourse. While many incidents of 'hate' target China, anti-Asian and anti-Semitic hate speech is also on the rise. Xenophobia around the pandemic has reportedly given rise to physical violence against people of Asian descent (see Jones, Section 2).

My interest here is not so much in documenting examples of hate speech around COVID-19 as to use COVID-19 as a way to understand how the idea of hate speech is discursively constructed. While the aforementioned examples may have been perceived as hate, hate speech as a concept has always been extremely contested and ambiguous. Nonetheless, COVID-19 has provided an opportunity for us to reflect on and problematize the complexity of hate speech, and to revisit the power of language and discourse in times of crisis. Doing so also situates hate speech in a particular moment in history, lending support to the overall approach to discourse this volume adopts.

Can Hate Speech Be Defined?

Hatred is one of the most common human emotions, and aggressive language has existed for centuries. Hate speech, however, is a relatively recent notion. According to the *Oxford English Dictionary*, hate speech was originally a US concept, first recorded use in 1938, but up until now, even in the US, there is no universally accepted definition. Nonetheless, there is at least a consensus that hate speech is speech that incites violence and discrimination against specific social groups. Existing definitions associate hate speech with categories of race, religion, gender and ethnicity, as defined by the United Nations and the UK government:

> Hate is defined as 'any kind of communication in speech, writing or behaviour, that attacks or uses pejorative or discriminatory language with reference to a person or a group'. (United Nations, 2019)
> The term 'hate crime' can be used to describe a range of criminal behaviour where the perpetrator is motivated by hostility or demonstrates hostility towards the victim's disability, race, religion, sexual orientation or transgender identity. (The Crown Prosecution Service, 2017)

In the USA, hate speech is protected free speech under the First Amendment, regardless of how offensive the content. Hate speech only becomes an issue when it is clearly coupled with direct action, resulting in violence or other forms of danger to others, which is judged on a case-by-case basis.

In reality, the line between free speech and hate speech remains blurry. Existing legal definitions are extremely vague and subject to interpretation. For example, what counts as hateful content or incitement of violence varies across contexts and cultures. What further complicates the matter is so-called 'soft' or covert hate speech, such as the use of metaphors and irony, which does not contain aggressive language, but through their connotations can cause an equal degree of harm to victims.

To further illustrate the complexity of hate speech, I now turn to what is perhaps one of the most debated topics around COVID-19 – the naming of the coronavirus. I provide a snapshot of how CDA can be employed to understand this issue as discursive action. The examples are taken from comments from various social media. Following the general principles of CDA, the content, context, discourse strategies and linguistic realizations are considered.

What's in a Name? Labelling COVID-19

The labelling of COVID-19 has sparked controversies since US President Donald Trump's repeated mentions of 'Chinese Virus' and 'China Virus' in various public appearances in March 2020, and later in June when he also referred to the virus as 'Kung flu' at his election rallies. On 7 May 7 2020, San Antonio City Council passed a resolution against the use of terms such as 'Chinese Virus' and 'Kung flu' to describe COVID-19, and declared that these are hate speech, a decision which US Senator Ted Cruz called 'nuts' (Aaro, 2020). In what follows, I describe my observations of some recurrent discourse strategies adopted by those commenters who are against racially charged labels of the virus and by those who defend this naming practice.

'Hate is a Virus ... '

Those who are against the name 'Chinese Virus' argue that the label incites further violence against Chinese and Asians online and offline. Two key discourse strategies have been identified in such anti-naming discourse:

(1) *Reference to authority*: The WHO is often cited as the authority of naming the virus SARS-CoV-2 and the disease which it causes COVID-19, as in the following comments from Twitter.

do us all a favor and read this **guidance from the @WHO** on naming diseases, & stop calling it 'Chinese Virus'.

That's why **WHO gives an official name COVID-19** to avoid racism, just use the right name!

This strategy is what Van Leeuwen (2007) refers to as 'impersonal authority', where actors refer to policy, regulation, law, organizations in defending their social action as acceptable.

(2) *Metaphors*: The virus metaphor has been widely used to negatively construct hate speech and racism as something as destructive as the virus. In the following Instagram posts, the 'virus' metaphor becomes a powerful tool to reframe abstract concepts such as hate and racism as something that is as concrete and vivid (and deadly) as the coronavirus.

Stop calling the illness the 'Chinese virus.' ... **Hate is a virus.** (Instagram)

stop the racism to Asian, **I AM NOT A VIRUS**. (Instagram) (See also Fig. 8.1)

'It's Not Racist at All ... '

At the same time, what has been considered hate or racism is justified by those who support the use of 'Chinese virus' through various legitimation discourse strategies. For a detailed account of legitimation strategies in CDA, see Van Leeuwen (2007).

(1) *Attributing to origin*: This is possibly the most common legitimation strategy in defending the term 'Chinese Virus'. When President Trump was asked why he repeatedly used the name at a press conference in March 2020, he said, 'It's not racist at all ... It comes from China, that's why.' The hashtag *#ItComesfromChina*, as an intertextual reference to Trump's words, immediately went viral on Twitter in the following week. By presenting the origin of the virus as a matter of fact, this justification strategy allows speakers to explain their action as free from prejudice and thus acceptable. By referring to Trump's words, the hashtag also draws on the strategy of 'authorization' (see (4) Authorization).

Figure 8.1 #IamNotAVirus (Photo credit: @JLSunW on Twitter, with permission from the owner)

(2) *Referring to antecedents*: Another common strategy of normalizing the use of 'Chinese virus' is to point readers to diseases that are named after countries or places, such as Spanish Flu and Hong Kong Flu. Others suggest that 'Wuhan Virus' was already in use in China before the official name SARS-CoV-2, for example, '*FYI. The term of #WuhanVirus (#武汉肺炎) is **quite common** in Chinese media since 1/2020*' (Twitter). Adjectives such as 'common' and 'normal' are effective in framing this naming practice as norm-conforming, thus downplaying the potentially racist comment.

(3) *Shared knowledge*: Arguments of this type justify the naming practice by framing it as shared common knowledge, as in the following tweet:

We all know that the virus is from Wuhan.

It is not racism #WuhanCoronavirus #ChineseCoronavirus' (Twitter).

This legitimation strategy is often realized by the factive verb 'know' or the phrase 'we know that' to project a factive presupposition. The pronoun 'we' is a common engagement device to construct common ground of knowledge with the audience. Doing so also seeks acceptance and support from a wider group.

(4) ***Authorization***: Authorization is a common legitimation strategy where speakers or writers draw on voices from authorities to enhance the credibility of their utterances and actions. In response to the banning of 'Chinese Virus' in San Antonio, some argued that this would seriously jeopardize freedom of speech, as in the following Twitter comments:

They are violating **the First Amendment**' (Twitter).

Check **case law and SCOTUS rulings**. Regardless, 'Chinese virus' is farrrrrrr from hate speech.

These are again examples of Van Leeuwen's 'impersonal authorization' which is realized through references to laws and regulations.

(5) *Claiming insider status*: Some commenters align themselves with victims' identity, as in the Twitter post: '***I'm Chinese***, *this disgusting virus is called #Chinesevirus ... **Not racist**.*' (Twitter). The commenter's self-positioning of 'I'm Chinese' further justifies their potentially controversial action of calling the virus 'Chinese virus'. The disclaimer at the end, 'Not racist' distances oneself from the underlying assumption that any alleged racist remarks are made by people of non-Chinese descent. Claiming their Chinese status adds further credibility to the controversial naming practice.

These discourse strategies may be used independently or in combination. These examples make clear that the meaning of hate speech and racism is constantly discursively constructed. It is often through social actors' redefinitions of these social problems that they become normalized.

Hate Speech and the Affective Public

Expressing hatred per se is not a crime. In pragmatics, there is a long tradition of recognizing 'expressive speech acts', which serve the function of expressing emotions, including anger. The advent of social media has given rise to the making of 'affective publics' (Papacharissi, 2015). Emotions have become mediatized as we increasingly engage in public online debates and express dissatisfaction about all sorts of social issues. Of course, verbal aggression is more than just an expressive speech act. In CDA, it is important to understand discursive actions within their broader historical and social contexts. In other words, expressions of anti-Chinese sentiment cannot be understood solely within the immediate context of COVID-19; we also need to consider the other relevant historical contexts where such sentiments have been repeatedly expressed.

Society has long equated hate speech with racism and discrimination, because hateful language does have the potential power to harm vulnerable social groups. However, 'hate speech' as a label is not unproblematic. When speech is premodified by 'hate', it immediately presupposes that it is something derogatory in nature and therefore must be banned, regardless of intent. However, banning hate speech may potentially restrict 'radicalist discourse' (i.e. 'language use by radical movements'), which often shares similar discourse strategies to what can easily be argued to be hate speech (Chiluwa, 2015: 218).

During the pandemic, hate speech has been framed as something as deadly as the virus. On 8 May 2020, United Nations Chief, António Guterres, appealed to the world to address and counter COVID-19 hate speech. He concluded his speech by saying: 'Let's defeat hate speech – and COVID-19 – together.' Unfortunately, hate speech will not just stop (Whillock, 2000). A number of media literacy campaigns have been launched to enhance people's awareness of the potential harm of all forms of aggressive behaviour online. The UNESCO has recently launched the 'End Xenophobia around COVID-19' campaign, with a long list of 'DOs and DON'Ts' to stop hate speech (Fig. 8.2).

What Can (Critical) Discourse Analysts Offer?

Language is powerful. Hateful language is particularly powerful. It works because it serves as a direct threat, a precursor to more explicit action (Whillock, 2000: 79).

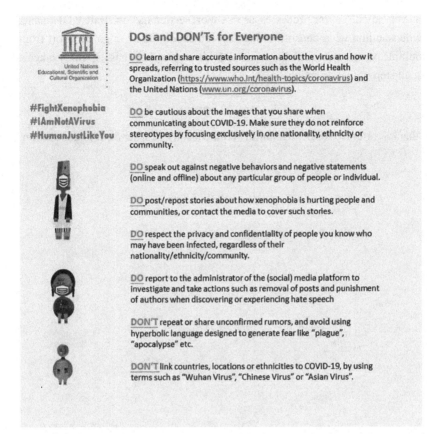

Figure 8.2 UNESCO's End Xenophobia campaign (unesco.org)

Racism against Asians is not exclusive to COVID-19. Any incidents of racism during the pandemic only echo this long-standing historical problem. We don't know whether a to-do list like the UNESCO's campaign will end hate speech. What we do know is, online aggression, as with any social action, largely manifests itself in language and discourse. Language researchers have a significant role to play in offering a better understanding of the linguistic realizations of online aggression by informing the public and policy makers about the overt and covert discourse strategies through which online aggression is enacted. We also need to understand the context and conditions that engender hate speech. Authentic interaction in which hate speech is evident should be analysed. Official and lay definitions of hate speech should be problematized. These can be achieved through applying tools and concepts of CDA.

Ultimately, it is people's attitudes that make a difference, not just laws and policies. What a (critical) discourse-analytic approach to hate speech can offer is a way to uncover the discourse strategies of online abuse that may be hidden in everyday discourse processes, as this short section has illustrated. Of course, understanding what constitutes hate speech should be an ongoing effort from multiple perspectives and disciplines. My discussion here has hopefully taken a small step in that direction.

Acknowledgments

I thank Jenifer Ho for her insightful comments on an earlier draft of this section.

9 Order out of Chaos: Coronavirus Communication and the Construction of Competence

Rodney H. Jones

During the first three months of the coronavirus epidemic in the UK, while over 30,000 people died from the virus, the government of Prime Minister Boris Johnson experimented with the design of the signs that appeared on the podiums at the government's daily briefings. They started off as just a URL (nhs.uk/coronavirus), but quickly changed to a three part slogan: 'Stay Home, Protect the NHS, Save Lives'. At first, one part of the slogan appeared on each of the three podiums, but that strategy perhaps led to uncomfortable deliberations about which minister got to stand behind each of the phrases (Fig. 9.1).

The solution was to put all three parts of the slogan together, but it took the government a while to figure out the best way to do that. At first, the phrases appeared displayed vertically one on top of the other (Fig. 9.2) in three colours that, at least partially aligned with the (ISO) International Organization for Standardization's design principles for safety signs and markings: yellow, which is normally used as a warning colour, for *Stay at Home*, and blue, which is often used for displaying vital or mandatory information, for *Protect the NHS*. The problem was that *Save Lives* was presented in red, the colour ISO recommends for communicating prohibition – talking about something

Figure 9.1 Prime Minister's statement on coronavirus, 20 March 2020 (source: www.gov.uk)

Figure 9.2 Government coronavirus briefing, 24 March 2020 (source www.gov.uk)

you're *not* supposed to do. Another problem was that the vertical arrangement of the three phrases on the podiums rendered the slogan practically illegible.

So, in its next iteration, the phrases were arranged horizontally (Fig. 9.3), which made it much easier to read, unless of course, you happened to be colour blind. But as soon as the government realized its mistake, they changed it again.

The next version is the one that survived up until early May, a yellow sign with red warning stripes that made the daily briefing resemble the scene of a traffic accident (Fig. 9.4)

While such decisions may seem trivial, the effective mobilization of different semiotic resources – from verbal slogans, to colours, to typographical styles – is crucial for successful health communication. Their importance, however, is not just a matter of communicating a clear message to the public, but also a matter of branding the overall campaign and creating a kind of public image for those who are delivering it.

Mediated discourse analysis is an approach to discourse which focuses on the *actions* that different kinds of discourse make possible, and the *social identities* people are able to claim or impute onto others through these actions. From the perspective of MDA, effective health communication is not just a matter of communicating information, but of deploying semiotic resources that empower people to take actions to protect themselves, and that help construct and sustain effective social practices and social identities around health and risk (Jones, 2013). If discourse is seen as a kind of scaffolding which allows people to perform actions and identities, then the main problem with an ineffective health message is not that people don't understand it, but that people don't know what to *do* with it.

Figure 9.3 Government coronavirus press conference, 25 March 2020 (source www.gov.uk)

Figure 9.4 Government coronavirus press conference, 3 April 2020 (source: www.gov.uk)

An example of this can be seen in a new slogan the government rolled out in May to mark a 'new phase' of its anti-COVID campaign: 'Stay Alert. Control the Virus, Save Lives' (Fig. 9.5).

Figure 9.5 Government COVID-19 slogan, 9 May 2020

Not only did the wording change, but also the colour. Instead of the red warning stripes, the stripes became green, which, according to the ISO should be used to communicate 'Safe. No action required'.

The government's new slogan quickly became the target of scathing criticism from the press and public before it even found its way onto the Prime Minster's podium. Dave Ward, general secretary of the Communication Workers Union, for example, remarked, 'Stay alert? It's a deadly virus not a zebra crossing' ('Coronavirus: Leaders unite … ', 2020), and author J. K. Rowling asked, 'Is coronavirus sneaking around in a fake moustache and glasses? If we drop our guard, will it slip us a Micky Finn? What the hell is 'stay alert' supposed to mean?' (Rowling, 2020). Within hours, social media was awash with parodies (Fig. 9.6):

According to *The Daily Telegraph*, the main impetus behind Downing Street's new slogan, 'Stay Alert' was the fear that the previous slogan to 'Stay Home' had proved too effective, and that the government was under increased pressure from employers to get people back on the job (Malnick, 2020). Here's where the parody shared by applied linguist Christian Chun seems particularly appropriate (Fig. 9.7; Chun, 2020):

What this particular parody highlights, at least from a mediated discourse analytical point of view, is that understanding the actions that are enabled by different semiotic resources can sometimes be rather complex, and different actions might be enabled for different kinds of people. For business owners, for example, the phrase 'stay alert' might be used as a way to compel their employees to return to work.

Rainbow Warriors

At the same time he unveiled the government's new slogan, the Prime Minister also announced a new *COVID-19 Alert System* consisting of five threat levels ranging from green (level one) to red (level five) (Fig. 9.8).

Figure 9.6 Parodies of government's slogan

Figure 9.7 Another parody

The system is based on the terror alert system, which uses a similar multicoloured scale, raising the question, what are the consequences of adopting a system used for terrorist alerts for health communication? What kinds of social actions and social identities does it enable or constrain?

One consequence, of course, is that it serves to reinforce the militaristic framing that has characterized the UK government's response to the crisis from the beginning: like terrorists, the virus is characterized as an 'invisible enemy' (see Jaworska, Section 5). A problem with this, though, is that terrorist alerts are directed *both* at the public and at terrorists themselves, designed to

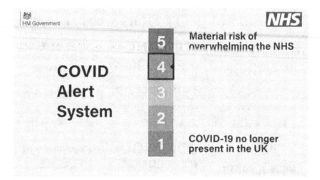

Figure 9.8 UK COVID-Alert System (source: NHS)

discourage them from carrying out attacks in the context of increased attention from law enforcement (Lehrke, 2016). It doesn't work that way with infectious diseases. (It is unlikely that the coronavirus watched the Prime Minister's address.) The most important question, however, remains: What does such a system allow the public (and the government) to *do* in response to the virus?

To assess how effective the COVID-alert system might be as a health communication tool, it's good to consider the terrorist alert system that it is modelled after. Britain's colour-coded terrorist alert system is based on a system instituted in the USA in 2002 called the US Homeland Security Advisory System, which was intended to communicate to the public the chances of a terrorist event, presumably in order to help people 'stay alert' and to tell them how alert they should stay. During the nine years the system was in operation in the States, however, the threat level didn't change much, mostly alternating between yellow ('significant' risk) and orange ('high' risk), and so the message it ended up sending was not particularly nuanced – basically, 'be scared … all the time' (Fig. 9.9).

At the time of its release, the system was widely ridiculed. The main criticisms were that it reduced something as multifaceted and complex as terrorism into a simple set of vague warnings (what's the difference between a 'significant' threat and a 'high' threat) and that it really did not give the public very clear guidance as to what to do when they received a terrorist alert other than 'stay alert'. The system didn't provide specific information about the exact nature of the threat (since that information was mostly classified) and didn't provide individuals with a concrete set of actions to take in response (Bonilla & Grimmer, 2013).

In the end, then, the system ended up having a detrimental effect on the US government's ability to communicate meaningfully with citizens about the threat of terrorism, mostly because it eroded trust in the government itself.

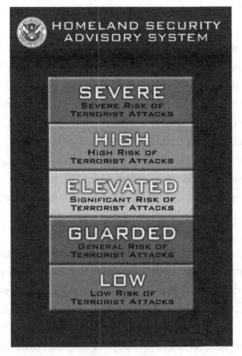

Figure 9.9 US Terror Alert System 2002–11

This lack of trust manifested most dramatically in accusations that President Bush was manipulating the system for political purposes when people noticed that elevations from yellow to orange correlated with downturns in his approval ratings. Meanwhile, studies conducted at the time showed that, while the alerts did increase people's perception of the likelihood of a terrorist attack, they had little impact on people's understanding of what they could do personally to keep themselves safe. Rather, the main results seemed to be increases in public pessimism about the economy and increases in the chances people would suffer from symptoms of anxiety and depression (McDermott & Zimbardo, 2006).

In 2011, the USA scrapped the system in favour of the new National Terrorism Advisory System (NTAS), which is still in use. In the new system, there are no colours and just two threat levels: 'elevated', for when the government has credible information regarding a terrorist attack and 'imminent' for when the information is especially specific. Also, in the new system, when an alert is issued, it includes information about steps individuals or communities should be taking to protect themselves and their families (Kirby, 2013).

In 2006, the UK unveiled its own version of the US system, partly based on a system that was already in place but had been restricted to government departments. In fact, one likely reason that the UK Threat Level system was rolled out for public use was that the government believed it would protect politicians and intelligence services from accusations that they were withholding crucial information from citizens, especially in the event that something went terribly wrong. But, like the American system, the UK Threat Level system has some worrying ambiguities, particularly in terms of how members of the public are meant to respond to various kinds of alerts. It is unclear for example, whether the correct response to a 'critical' threat level is for the public to avoid certain areas, to monitor the media for further information, or to go about business as usual. As a result, such alerts seem to have little impact on public behaviour.

The way the five levels of the system are labelled is also problematic given how similar some of the words are in meaning. The words used for the top three levels – 'critical', 'severe' and 'substantial' – are essentially synonyms for most people. Such ambiguity can actually desensitize the public to the whole notion of a 'threat' and feed into cynical theories that the government is only trying to 'cover itself' by constantly keeping the country at a high level of alert.

If you're looking for clarity about what you are actually supposed to do while staying alert, you might check the website of the Security Service (2020) where you would learn that actually you're not supposed to do anything other than remain 'vigilant'. Under the heading, *How should you respond?* the website advises:

> Threat levels in themselves do not require specific responses from the public. They are a tool for security practitioners working across different sectors of the Critical National Infrastructure (CNI) and the police to use in determining what protective security response may be required. Vigilance is vital regardless of the current national threat level. It is especially important given the current national threat. Sharing national threat levels with the general public keeps everyone informed.

In other words – 'stay alert'.

The bottom line is, colour-coded alert systems are simply not very effective ways of alerting people to threats. It is not surprising, then that, since its unveiling in May, the government's national colour-coded COVID-Alert system has all but disappeared from public discourse. The threat level is not updated on a government website or announced daily by the BBC or projected onto a big screen in Piccadilly Circus. Most people, I dare say, would have no idea what the current national threat level is. In October, the Prime Minister added to the national alert system local alert levels in an effort to 'simplify' communication, but these only served to further muddy the waters, especially when disputes broke out between the Prime Minster and local authorities about what sorts of restrictions should accompany the different tiers. In response to this new alert system, Dr Carina J. Fearnley, Director of the UCL Warning Research Centre, said:

> I'm not convinced that this new local system will be enough to offset previous failures. There was no mention of the national COVID alert level systems in the recent announcement, so it is not clear how these two systems work together, or if the broader system is now defunct. Why is the UK government continually revising and changing its alert systems? Why is this information still not clear and transparent? (Fearnly & Smith, 2020)

Conclusion

It seems that the most important function of the slogans, logos and colour-coded alert system that the UK has deployed to combat the coronavirus is that it provides a kind of scaffolding upon which the Prime Minister and his government can stage their performance of competence. For example, although the COVID-alert system has not proven to be a particularly useful tool for communicating about risk to the general public, it has proved to be a useful performative tool for the government. The next time the national alert level was mentioned after the initial announcement was on 19 June, when Health Secretary Matt Hancock announced that it had been reduced from 4 to 3. While there were no immediate policy changes accompanying the announcement, Hancock did take the opportunity to tout the new number as proof that what the government was doing was working, characterizing it as 'a big moment for the country' (Wooller & Mullin, 2020). So, even though the number doesn't communicate much to the public about what they should do, it does serve to assure them that what the government is doing is right. The alert level was then raised back to 4 in September, with rather less fanfare.

The main problem with the government's use of alert systems is that, by trying to dress up what is essentially vague advice in the discourse of precision, it actually ends up constraining rather than enabling effective action against the pandemic. The illusion of precision, in fact, is even more dangerous than the vagueness of the threat levels and the advice associated with them. Studies of terrorist threat systems (e.g. Bausch et al., 2013), for instance, show that when people think advice seems precise and scientific, they are actually *more* likely to take unnecessary risks.

By saying that the Prime Minister is using this elaborate colour-coded system as a way to *manufacture competence*, I don't mean to be insulting or to imply that he lacks actual competence. Policy communication *requires* the discursive construction of competence in order to win support from the public. But without providing the public with clear tools with which to take action, performances of competence fail as health communication messages.

10 How to Make Sense of Communication and Interaction in a Pandemic*

Elisabetta Adami

Since mid-February 2020, when I first heard that the coronavirus pandemic had started to hit Northern Italy (where my parents are based) and sensed it was heading for to the UK (where I am based), I have perceived a sense of urgency in trying to make sense of the implications of this crisis for our social lives. As Rodney writes so profoundly well in the Introduction of this Element, I too was struggling, constantly asking myself how a social semiotician like me could ever be of any use in the midst of a global emergency where keeping people alive was the priority. I did not have it fully clear at that time, but I somehow felt that the effects of the pandemic on communication and social interaction were significant and important to understand.

While my private interactions and the posts on my social media feeds from people based in different countries started to look strikingly similar in terms of both themes and issues of contestation, I felt the need to record, trace and reflect on what I was observing and experiencing. I started to take notes of my perceptions, behaviours and interactions with others, to screenshot social media posts, and bookmark articles that I was coming across.

Frustratingly, this whole process was extremely chaotic and limited – what I was capturing, through my personal window on the situation, was partial and very fragmented, and while the situation was changing rapidly, I was struggling to keep track of it all and felt I needed to network with others to construct a wider picture.

At the same time, I was also noticing that, like me, everybody else was constantly observing, reflecting, trying to make sense of – and commenting on – the situation. Observations, self-reflections and commentaries were not only about the virus, but also – and often – about behaviours – ways of conducting oneself and interacting with others, both online and offline. They were, in sum, about sign- and meaning-making practices. This, I thought, is something that social semioticians like me can help to make sense of.

My observations, notes and reflections in the first couple of months since mid-February 2020 pointed to a changing semiotic regime, as the combinatory possibilities between media, meaning-making resources, places, times and roles of everyday activities were being reshuffled (Adami, 2020). Everybody was sensing it, and everybody's insights and perspectives were

---

* This is necessarily a condensed report. For a more nuanced discussion, you can refer to my article published in the PanMeMic website (Adami, 2020), and the PanMeMic Manifesto, coauthored by members of PanMeMic on behalf of the whole founding team (Adami et al., 2020).

extremely useful to help construct a wider picture. So, with other colleagues worldwide, we came up with a Manifesto that reworked these coordinates of a changing semiotic regime into four main factors and four key dimensions of change, together with a call for everybody to contribute (Adami et al., 2020).

The Coordinates of a Changing Semiotic Regime

Four interrelated factors make the changes in communication and social interaction unprecedented:

1 **The human body as the centre of danger, with the need to keep bodies apart to keep them safe**: Given that bodies are humans' primary medium for interacting with the world and others, policies to keep bodies apart radically affect our social practices.
2 **The available communication infrastructure to keep people connected (and productive)**: Compensating for the separation of bodies, the digital re-mediation of all kinds of social activities online has also radically affected how we do things, while online communication systems have enabled instant and distant information sharing and discussion.
3 **The character of the changes: Abrupt** – as the immediate danger has imposed urgency; **pervasive** – as changes affect very basic movements and actions (i.e. the 'how to do things') in all domains and spheres of social life, both in our physical environments, because of the separation of bodies, and online for the digital remediation of activities to keep societies functioning; **global** – as changes have affected everybody to a certain extent, and our communication system has made us perceive it even more so; and **totalizing** – as for months this has been the sole or main concern in all forms of communication.
4 **A re-disciplining process**: Because of all the above, habituated practices and behaviours are no longer safe or viable; people have had to reconsider, replan and recreate ways in which they conduct activities, interact with others and manage space. We have been re-disciplining ourselves, unlearning automated movements, actions and practices while co-constructing new, safe and viable ones. The abrupt and pervasive re-disciplining process is energy consuming and stressful, but carries with it a heightened awareness. What was habituated and familiar before can no longer take place, while new practices are emerging and being attempted in the making. As these have not been naturalized yet, a heightened awareness of our actions offers a unique opportunity for (self-)reflection – hence the need and urgency for making the best of the distributed knowledge networks that are being developed to

understand the ongoing changes, before new practices are habituated and the potential for self-reflection is heavily diminished.

Driven by those interrelated factors, four key dimensions of communication and interaction are undergoing changes:

1 **Mediation:** With bodies needing to be kept apart, the metaphor of the bubble has migrated from online environments to interactions in the physical world, and screens have become our windows on the world and to others. Limitation of physical mobility has been compensated by remediating all sorts of activities online, in all spheres of life. This has contributed to heightening the inequalities and dynamics of social exclusion produced by the so-called digital divide. It has also produced a considerable digital learning curve – an explosion of creativity in formulating practices to compensate for the absence of embodied co-presence, as well as a potential transnational widening of people's activities (through participation in online events based somewhere else). Other effects include an increased calendarization and datafication of social life, risks for privacy and potentially diminished chances for social serendipity.

2 **Channels of perceptions:** With touch and close proximity no longer safe outside the households and not afforded online, the auditory and visual channels of perception have taken on a predominant role in communication and interaction with others. The ruling out of close bodily co-presence, both in physical interaction and online, has potentially significant – and still not fully known – perceptive, cognitive and affective consequences for everybody, and particularly for those social groups, individuals and roles that rely more on close proximity and/or touch. It also carries with it heightened challenges for people with sensory impairments.

3 **Semiotic resources and meaning-making practices:** Changes in mediation and in viable channels of perception have impacted on the semiotic resources used to make meaning – the dominant ones now being those relying on auditory and visual channels. Online remediation and physical distance between bodies, together with the wearing of masks, have an impact on the use of gaze, gesture and body proxemics, as well as on speech, challenged while wearing masks and strictly regulated in multiparty interactions online, so that new strategies need to be adopted. Touching or coming close to others are potentially resignified (from communicating closeness to potential signs of threat), while new online practices are emerging as a larger number of people participate and new types of activities are digitally re-mediated. We have been undergoing a 'reshuffling of associations between signifiers and signifieds, while points of references between old social practices and

emerging safer ones are collapsing, and there is a potential constant reassess-
ment and reshuffling of the identities people intentionally "give" and the ones
they "give off" (Gottman, 1959)' (Adami et al., 2020: 9).

4 **Interaction order:** The spheres and domains of private and public have
   undergone a stark separation in our physical environments – with a marked
   threshold between home and public space, the crossing of which requires us
   to re-discipline ourselves, from basic movements and actions to all kinds of
   habituated practices. At the same time, private and public have invaded each
   other through what is shown on our screens, with all kinds of activities taking
   place online from home. This has, at the same time, produced a confusion or
   reshuffling of former markers of formality and informality.

As we have been undergoing an at-least-momentary collapse of semiotic
regimes (that is, established patterns of association between forms and meanings), and we have all been going about interpreting and co-constructing new
practices, we find ourselves at a key moment to observe these dynamics and
assess what is gained and what is lost (Kress, 2005), and to predict the implications for our future social lives.

The question for me then has been how to do so, given that (1) while the
changes are global, they are taking place in an extremely socially diverse and
unequal world, and that (2) there is an urgency of capturing sensations, reflections, fears and experiences before practices are naturalized and while there is
still time to voice concerns about and impact the direction of change. The
phenomenon is simply too broad, too diverse and multifaceted, and too fleeting
and changing to use the traditional methods of data collection and analysis that
I, as a social semiotic discourse and interactional analyst, am familiar with.

PanMeMic: Towards Public, Live and Conversational Collective Semiotic Research beyond Academia

The urgency to make sense, combined with the awareness that my experience is
partial, and that there is a general tendency to observe and reflect on changes,
led me to contact thirty colleagues worldwide to set up *PanMeMic (Pandemic
Meaning Making of Interaction and Communication)*. We launched the project
in mid May 2020 as a transnational collective research experience/experiment.
It uses the affordances of social media to involve both academics and non-
academics in reflections and conversations with everybody interested in how
the pandemic is changing the ways in which we communicate and interact with
others.

PanMeMic is a transmedia space spanning a website (https://panmemic.hypoth
eses.org/) and several social media accounts (including Facebook, Instagram,

Twitter, WeChat, WeiBo and YouTube). Although still in its infancy at the time of writing, PanMeMic intends to initiate an innovative research approach and set of methods, inspired by citizen science, that can complement existing approaches and methods in (social) semiotics, multimodal studies and interactional sociolinguistics. It does so by involving academics and non-academics in public, open and live forms of reflection and discussion, to understand changes in communication and social interaction, how they affect different persons, as well as the fears and problems people are facing, and the resources they put in place, together with the possibilities for impacting these changes.

The methodological innovation draws on (1) the Socratic tradition, in pursuing understanding through public and live conversations, which can now be traceable by using the affordances of social media, and on (2) citizen science (www.citizenscience.org/; for reviews see Kullenberg & Kasperowski 2016; Lewenstein 2016), involving non-academics in the co-construction of knowledge (for participatory research in the humanities and social sciences, see Facer and Pahl, 2017; for disability studies, see Watson et. al. 2012; for a crowd-sourced research project on the pandemic in anthropology, see https://anthro covid.com/; for citizen sociolinguistics, see Rymes 2020; Rymes & Leone 2014; Svendsen 2018).

In only two months (18 May – 17 July 2020), the PanMeMic website has published 12 articles, attracting 4,536 unique visitors (for a total of 7,907 visits) and 42 comments; the social media accounts have engaged over 1,300 people; the PanMeMic Facebook group reached 746 members, with 242 posts, 731 comments and 3,384 reactions. Table 10.1 shows the range of topics discussed in the Facebook group, derived through a preliminary thematic analysis of the posts in the Facebook group (achieved by assigning only one theme to each post, without considering the comments).

The sharing of observations and pictures, reflections on one's own practices, requests for advice and links to news items in the posts trigger comments from people based in other countries that often widen the perspective, 'generating transnational exchanges that give a sense of the complex intertwining between sharedness and specificities of the global phenomenon for each given topic being discussed, thus enriching the individual's positionality and understanding in a way that would not be possible otherwise' (Adami et al., 2020: 16).

As people post their reflections and observations, ask for advice, share their fears and provide suggestions of practices they've developed or adopted, the conversations generated in this first spontaneous phase of the project can offer insights onto how semiotic knowledge is co-constructed while practices are emerging. Understanding how distributed semiotic knowledge in-the-making develops (along the lines of what Rymes' 2020 citizen sociolinguistic research

Table 10.1 List of topics of the PanMeMic Facebook group posts – 18 May–17 July 2020.

Ads	Fears	Online gigs	Smiles
Anti-COVID parties	Food	Painting	Snowmen
App visuals	Gaze	Parody	Socializing
Arab response	Gestures	Paths	Software updates
Architecture	Greetings	Play	Solidarity
Black lives matter	Gyms	Political discourse	Soundscape
Bodies in space	Hairstyles	Political posters	Space
Borders	Head protections	Populism	Spiritual growth
Branding	Health costs	PPEs	Stores
Calls	Hearing impairment	Products and Services	Street art
Campus life	Home spaces	Protests	Surgeons
Children's language	Hugs	Public communication	Teaching
Children's art craft	Infographics	Public policing behaviour	TikTok
Comics	Kindness and surveillance	Public signs	Touch
Dance	Language	Public transport	Toys
Digital learning	Loneliness	Queue	Travels
Drive-ins	Masks	Rainbow	TV shows
Eid's cards	Memes	Rave culture	US
Elections	Music	Redesign of places	Videocalls

does for language practices) is key well beyond this historical moment. As a next step in the project, in-depth analysis of these open conversations on such an extremely wide range of topics (as illustrated in Table 10.1), generated organically out of a period of heightened awareness and meta-reflection, might provide insights into broader social-semiotic dynamics of meaning making, and of co-construction and distribution of practices.

This collective research experience is still in its infancy and has so far developed on an entirely voluntary and spontaneous basis. Next steps will involve developing methods to assess the knowledge produced as well as more structured forms of inquiry. Admittedly, at least at the moment, the design of these next steps raises more questions than it provides answers.

In the meantime, I have been learning a lot from the shared reflections and conversations taking place in this collective research space, in a way that I would hardly have otherwise. One key thing I have learned, well beyond the pandemic, is that we may need to (re-)ask ourselves what counts as semiotic research, how it is done, who has expertise for doing it and what the boundaries are between data and anecdotal accounts when it comes to inherently human practices and experiences such as communication and interaction. Hopefully, by continuing these collective forms of discussion, we will be able to find answers that are suitable for these changing times.

References

Aaro, D. (2020, May 8). Ted Cruz slams San Antonio plan declaring 'Chinese virus' to be hate speech: 'This is NUTS'. *Fox News*. Accessed 6 May 2020, www.foxnews.com/politics/ted-cruz-slams-san-antonio-plan-declaring-chinese-virus-to-be-hate-speech-this-is-nuts.

Adami, E. (2020, May 19). How, where and who will we meet and hug again? And why this matters. Understanding communication in a global pandemic and the future of social interaction – Towards a collective semiotics. *PanMeMic*. Accessed 20 August 2020, https://panmemic.hypotheses.org/114

Adami, E., Al Zidjaly N., Canale G., et al. (2020). PanMeMic Manifesto: Making meaning in the Covid-19 pandemic and the future of social interaction. Working Papers in Urban Language and Literacies no. 273. Accessed 20 August 2020, https://f-origin.hypotheses.org/wp-content/blogs.dir/8699/files/2020/08/WP273_Adami_et_al_on_behalf_of_the_PanMe.pdf

Antanasova, D., & Koteyko, N. (2017). Obesity frames and counter-frames in British and German online newspapers. *Health*, 21(6): 650–69.

Assimakopoulos, S. 2020. Incitement to discriminatory hatred, illocution and perlocution. *Pragmatics and Society*, 11(2), 177–95.

Austin, J. L. (1975). *How to do things with words*. Oxford: Oxford University Press.

Backhaus, P. (2006). Multilingualism in Tokyo: A look into the linguistic landscape. *International Journal of Multilingualism*, 3(1), 52–66.

Baker, P. (2006). *Using corpora in discourse analysis*. London: Continuum.

Bausch, A. W., Faria, J. R., & Zeitzoff, T. (2013). Warnings, terrorist threats and resilience: A laboratory experiment. *Conflict Management and Peace Science*, 30(5), 433–51.

Ben-Rafael, E., Shohamy, E., Hasan Amara, M., & Trumper-Hecht, N. (2006). Linguistic landscape as symbolic construction of the public space: The case of Israel. *International Journal of Multilingualism*, 3(1), 7–30.

Bhatia, V. K. (1993). *Analyzing genre: Language use in professional settings*. London: Longman.

Bhatia, V. K. (2004). *Worlds of written discourse: A genre-based view*. London: Continuum.

Blommaert, J. (2020). COVID19 and globalization. Accessed 12 May 2020, https://alternative-democracy-research.org/2020/03/06/covid19-and-globalization/

Blommaert, J., & Backus, A. (2013). Superdiverse repertoires and the individual. In I. De Saint-Georges & J.-J. Weber (eds.), *Multilingualism and multimodality:*

Current challenges for educational studies (pp. 11–32). Rotterdam: Sense Publishers.

Bonilla, T., & Grimmer, J. (2013). Elevated threat levels and decreased expectations: How democracy handles terrorist threats. *Poetics*, *41*(6), 650–69.

Boroff, D. (2020, March 31). Cop pulls over doctor for speeding but gives her his coronavirus masks instead of a ticket. *The Sun*. Accessed 2 April 2020, www.thesun.co.uk/news/11291749/cop-pulls-over-doctor-for-speeding-but-gives-her-his-coronavirus-masks-instead-of-a-ticket/

Bosh, K., (2020). A marine biologist friend working from home due to coronavirus [digital image]. [Viewed 6 October 2020]. www.facebook.com/photo .php?fbid=3273060779389601&set=gm.3173374926058875&type=3&thea ter&ifg=1

Cenoz, J., & Gorter, D. (2006). Linguistic landscape and minority languages. *International Journal of Multilingualism*, *3*(1), 67–80.

Chan, Y. W. (2020, March 31). Mask or no mask: Is culture the reason for differing doctor's advice? *South China Morning Post*. Accessed April 2 2020, www.scmp.com/comment/opinion/article/3077558/mask-or-no-mask-cultural-assumptions-heart-coronavirus-crisis

Chiluwa, I. (2015). Radicalist discourse: a study of the stances of Nigeria's Boko Haram and Somalia's Al Shabaab on Twitter. *Journal of Multicultural Discourses*, 10(2), 214–35.

Choi, C. (2020, March 24). Fearing new round of coronavirus, mask-wearing Hong Kong targets barefaced foreigners. *Los Angeles Times*. Accessed 2 April 2020, www.latimes.com/world-nation/story/2020–03-24/you-might-get-shamed-for-wearing-a-mask-in-california-but-in-asia-its-the-opposite

Chun, C. (2020) Facebook comment. Accessed 11 May 2020, www.facebook .com/photo.php?fbid=10156751980630670&set=p.10156751980630670 &type=3&theater

Coronavirus: Leaders unite against PM's 'stay alert' slogan. (2020, 10 May) *Sky News*. Accessed 11 May 2020, https://news.sky.com/story/stay-alert-the-gov ernments-new-coronavirus-slogan-falls-flat–11985891

Dawkins R. (1976). *The selfish gene*. Oxford: Oxford University Press

Dorfman, L., & Wallack, L. (2007). Moving nutrition upstream: the case for reframing obesity. *Journal of Nutrition Education and Behavior*, 39(2): 45–50.

Dressen-Hammouda, D. (2008). From novice to disciplinary expert: Disciplinary identity and genre mastery. *English for Specific Purposes*, *27* (2), 233–52.

Dynel, M. (2016). 'I has seen image macros!' Advice animal memes as visual-verbal jokes. *International Journal of Communication*, *10*, 660–88.

Facer, K., & Pahl, K. (eds.). (2017). *Valuing interdisciplinary collaborative research: Beyond impact*. Bristol: Bristol University Press.

Fearnly, C. J., & Smith, D. (2020, October 17). Government's tiered Covid alert systems are all flawed says expert. Accessed 18 November 2020, WalesOnline website: www.walesonline.co.uk/news/uk-news/disaster-expert-says-uk-governments–19120253

Firth, J. R. (1957). Modes of meaning. In *Papers in linguistics* (pp. 1934–51). London, New York: Oxford University Press.

godoftitsandmemes., (2020). [Me after washing my hands for 20 seconds for 57 times a day] [digital image]. Viewed [6 October 2020]. www.instagram.com/p/B9nOQjdAxky/

Goffman, E. (1959). *The presentation of self in everyday life*. London: Penguin.

Gogonas, N., & Maligkoudi, C. (2019). Translanguaging instances in the Greek linguistic landscape in times of crisis. *Journal of Applied Linguistics*, 32, 66–82.

Grey, A. (2020, June 1). How to improve Australia's public health messaging about Covid-19. Language on the move. Accessed 3 June 2020, www.languageonthemove.com/how-to-improve-australias-public-health-messaging-about-covid–19/

Hafner, C. A. (2010). A multi-perspective genre analysis of the barrister's opinion: Writing context, generic structure, and textualization. *Written Communication*, 27(4), 410–41.

Hafner, C. A. (2013). The discursive construction of professional expertise: Appeals to authority in barrister's opinions. *English for Specific Purposes*, *32*(3), 131–43.

Halliday, M.A.K. (1978). *Language as social semiotic*. London: Edward Arnold.

Haynes, N. (2019). Extreme speech/writing on the walls: Discourses on Bolivian Immigrants in Chilean meme humor. *International Journal of Communication*, *13*, 3122–3142.

Heymann, D. (2020, April 3). Do face masks protect against coronavirus? Here's what scientists know so far. *The Guardian*. Accessed 6 April 2020, www.theguardian.com/commentisfree/2020/apr/03/face-masks-coronavirus-scientists-evidence-covid-19-public

Ho, W. Y. J., & Li, W. (2019). Mobilizing learning: A translanguaging view. *Chinese Semiotic Studies* 15 (4): 533–59.

Hodge, R., & Kress, G. (1988). *Social semiotics*. Cambridge: Polity Press.

Hopkyns, S. (2020, July 17). Linguistic diversity and inclusion in the era of COVID-19 Language on the move. Accessed 20 July 2020, www.langua

geonthemove.com/linguistic-diversity-and-inclusion-in-the-era-of-covid–19/

Hyland, K. (2005). *Metadiscourse: Exploring interaction in writing*. London: Continuum.

Hyland, K. (2010). Constructing proximity: Relating to readers in popular and professional science. *Journal of English for Academic Purposes*, *9*(2), 116–27.

Iedema, R. (2003). Multimodality, resemiotization: Extending the analysis of discourse as multi-semiotic practice. *Visual Communication* 2(1), 29–54.

imgflip.com, (2020a). *Corn teen* [digital image]. [Viewed 6 October 2020]. https://imgflip.com/i/3tq82t

imgflip.com, (2020b). *Corona Virus* [digital image]. [Viewed 6 October 2020]. https://imgflip.com/i/3n4ejq

Jaworska, S., and Leuschner, T. (2018). Crossing languages – crossing discourses: a corpus-assisted discourse study of Kulturkampf in German, Polish and English. *Pragmatics and Society*, 9(1), 119–149.

Jewitt, C. (2016). Multimodal analysis. In A. Georgakopoulou & T. Spilioti (eds.), *Handbook of language and digital communication* (pp.69–84). Abingdon: Routledge.

Jones, R. H. (2013). *Health and risk communication: An applied linguistic perspective*. London: Routledge.

Kirby, P. (2013). The end of the rainbow?: Terrorism and the future of public warning. *The RUSI Journal*, *158*(4), 54–60.

Klein, E. (2020, April 3). What social solidarity demands of us in a pandemic (Interview with Eric Klinenberg). *Vox*. Accessed 5 April 2020, www.vox .com/podcasts/2020/4/3/21204412/coronavirus-covid-19-pandemic-social-distancing-social-solidarity-the-ezra-klein-show

Kress, G. (2005). Gains and losses: New forms of texts, knowledge and learning. *Computer Composition*, 22, 4–22.

Kress, G. (2010). *Multimodality: A social semiotic approach to contemporary communication*. London: Routledge.

Kress, G., & van Leeuwen, T. (2006). *Reading images: The grammar of visual design* (2nd ed.). London: Routledge.

Kuiper, G. (2020). Ethnographic fieldwork quarantined. *Social Anthropology*, 28 (2), 300–301.

Kullenberg, C., & Kasperowski, D. (2016). What is citizen science? A scientometric meta-analysis. *PLoS ONE* 11: e0147152.

Lehrke, J. P. (2016). Terrorism alerts and target transference: Evidence and implications from the 2010 Europe-wide terrorism alert. *European Security*, *25*(1), 3–27.

Leuschner, T., & Jaworska, S. (2018). Anglo-German discourse crossings and contrasts: Introduction to the special issue. *Pragmatics & Society*, 9 (1), 2–7.

Lewenstein, B. V. (2016). Editorial: Can we understand citizen science? [Special Issue on Citizen Science]. *JCOM: Journal of Science Communication*, *14*, 1–5.

Li, W. (2011). Moment analysis and translanguaging space: Discursive construction of identities by multilingual Chinese youth in Britain. *Journal of Pragmatics* 43 (5),1222–1235.

Li, W. (2018). Translanguaging as a practical theory of language. *Applied Linguistics*, 39 (1), 9–30.

Li, W., & Ho, W. Y. J. (2018). Language learning sans frontiers: A translanguaging view. *Annual Review of Applied Linguistics*, *38*, 33–59.

Li W. & Zhu. (2020). Making sense of handwritten signs in public spaces. *Social Semiotics*. Published online at https://doi.org/10.1080/10350330.2020 .1810549

Lou, J. J. (2016). *The linguistic landscape of Chinatown: A sociolinguistic ethnography*. Bristol: Multilingual Matters.

Lynteris, C. (2018). Plague masks: The visual emergence of anti-epidemic personal protection equipment. *Medical Anthropology*, *37*(6), 442–457.

makeameme.org (2020a). [Quarantini] [digital image]. [Viewed 6 October 2020]. https://makeameme.org/meme/quarantini-its-just

makeameme.org (2020b). [Quaran-teen] [digital image]. [Viewed 6 October 2020]. https://makeameme.org/meme/quaran-teen

makeameme.org (2020c). [Coronials] [digital image]. [Viewed 6 October 2020]. https://makeameme.org/meme/in-9-to

makeameme.org (2020d). [Covidiot] [digital image]. [Viewed 6 October 2020]. https://makeameme.org/meme/covidiot-someone-who

Malnick, E. (2020, May 9). Stay alert: Boris Johnson's new message to the nation. *The Telegraph*. Accessed 11 May 2020, www.telegraph.co.uk/polit ics/2020/05/09/stay-alert-boris-johnsons-new-message-nation/

Mamadouh, V. (2018). Transient linguistic landscapes of activism. In P. A. Kraus & F. Grin (eds.), *The politics of multilingualism: Europeanisation, globalisation and linguistic governance* (Studies in World Language Problems 6; pp. 111–142). Amsterdam: John Benjamins.

Mauss, M. (1966). *The gift: The form and reason for exchange in Archaic societies*. London: Cohen & West.

McDermott, R., & Zimbardo, P. G. (2006) The psychological consequences of terrorist alerts. In B. Bongar, L.M. Brown, L.E. Beutler, J.N. Breckenridge & P.G. Zimbardo (eds.), *Psychology of terrorism* (pp. 357–70) Oxford University Press.

Milner, R. (2016). *The world made meme: Public conversations and participatory media*. Cambridge, MA: MIT Press.

Miltner, K. M., (2014). 'There's no place for lulz on LOLCats'. The role of genre, gender, and group identity in the interpretation and enjoyment of an Internet meme. *First Monday, 19*(8). https://doi.org/10.5210/fm.v19i8.5391

moonshot (2020, April 29). COVID-19: Conspiracy theories, hate speech and incitements to violence on Twitter. Accessed 6 May 2020, http://moonshotcve.com/covid-19-conspiracy-theories-hate-speech-twitter/

Otheguy, R., García, O., & Reid W. (2015). Clarifying translanguaging and deconstructing named languages: A perspective from linguistics. *Applied Linguistics Review* 6 (3): 281–304.

Oxford English Dictionary (OED). (2020). Corpus analysis of the language of Covid-19. Accessed 15 November 2020, https://public.oed.com/blog/corpus-analysis-of-the-language-of-covid-19/#note1

Papacharissi, Z. 2015. *Affective publics: Sentiment, technology, and politics*. Oxford University Press.

Parkinson, J., & Adendorff, R. (2004). The use of popular science articles in teaching scientific literacy. *English for Specific Purposes, 23*(4), 379–396.

Partington, A., Duguid, A., & Taylor, C. (2013). *Patterns and meanings in discourse. Theory and practice in corpus-assisted discourse studies (cads)*. Amsterdam: Benjamins.

Penney, J. (2019). 'It's so hard not to be funny in this situation': Memes and humor in US youth online political expression. *Television & New Media, 21*(8), 791–806.

Piata, A. (2016). When metaphor becomes a joke: Metaphor journeys from political ads to internet memes. *Journal of Pragmatics, 106*, 39–57.

plavonk., (2020). *Trump Virus* [digital image] [Viewed 6 October 2020]. https://imgflip.com/i/3r74q3

Pollock, D. (1995). Masks and the semiotics of identity. *The Journal of the Royal Anthropological Institute, 1*(3), 581–597.

Ravelli, L. J., & van Leeuwen, T. (2018). Modality in the digital age. *Visual Communication, 17*(3), 277–294.

Reisigl, M., & Wodak, R., 2005. *Discourse and discrimination: Rhetorics of racism and antisemitism*. Routledge.

Renwick, D. (2020, April 2). Face masks: Can they slow coronavirus spread – and should we be wearing them? *The Guardian*. Accessed 6 April 2020, www.theguardian.com/world/2020/apr/02/face-masks-coronavirus-covid-19-public

Rowling, J. K. (2020, 9 May) Tweet. Accessed 11 May 2020, https://twitter.com/jk_rowling/status/1259229863086612480/photo/1

Rymes, B. (2020). *How we talk about language: Exploring citizen sociolinguistics*. Cambridge: Cambridge University Press.

Rymes, B., & Leone, A. R. (2014). Citizen sociolinguistics: A new media methodology for understanding language and social life. *Working Papers in Educational Linguistics*, 29, 25–43.

Schröter, M. (2018). How words behave in other languages: The use of German Nazi vocabulary in English. *Pragmatics and Society*, 9(1), 93–118.

Scollon, R. (2002). What's the point? Can mediated discourse analysis stop the war? Accessed 18 April 2003, http://www.gutenbergdump.net/mdp/point .htm (no longer available)

Scollon, R., and Scollon, S. W. (2003). *Discourses in place: Language in the material world*. New York: Routledge.

secretNinja (2020). [Rona] [digital image]. [Viewed 6 October 2020]. http:// memerscommunity.com/quarantine-meme/

Security Service (UK) (2020). Threat levels. Accessed on 11 May 2020, www .mi5.gov.uk/threat-levels.

Semino, E., Demjen, Z., & Demmen, J. E. (2018). An integrated approach to metaphor and framing in cognition, discourse and practice, with an application to metaphors for cancer. *Applied Linguistics*, 39(5), 625–645.

Shifman, L. (2014). *Memes in digital culture*. Cambridge, MA: MIT Press.

Shohamy, E., & Gorter, D. (eds.). (2009). *Linguistic landscape: Expanding the scenery*. London: Routledge.

skywalk3r (2020). [Staying alive] [digital image]. [Viewed 6 October 2020]. https://imgur.com/gallery/52ayW4f

Sontag, S. (1989). *AIDS and its metaphors*. New York: Farrar, Straus and Giroux.

Stilgoe, J., Lock, S. J., and Wilsdon, J. (2014). Why should we promote public engagement with science? *Public Understanding of Science*, 23(1), 4–15.

Stubbs, M. (2001). Words and phrases: Corpus studies in lexical *semantics*. Blackwell, Oxford.

Suls, J. (1972). A two-stage model for the appreciation of jokes and cartoons: an information processing analysis. In J. Goldstein and P. McGhee (eds.), *The Psychology of Humor*, (pp. 81–100). New York: Academic Press.

Svendsen, B. A. (2018). The dynamics of citizen sociolinguistics. *Journal of Sociolinguistics*, 22(2), 137–160.

Swales, J. M. (1990). *Genre analysis: English in academic and research settings*. Cambridge: Cambridge University Press.

Taecharungroj, V., & Nueangjamnong, P. (2015). Humour 2.0: Styles and types of humour and virality of memes on Facebook. *Journal of Creative Communications*, 10(3), 288–302.

The Crown Prosecution Service (2017). Hate crime. Accessed 3 May 2020, www.cps.gov.uk/hate-crime

The Editorial Board (2020, March 23). Opinion: Call it 'coronavirus'. *The New York Times*. Accessed 24 March 2020, www.nytimes.com/2020/03/23/opinion/china-coronavirus-racism.html

The Shining Memes (2020). [Isolation with family] [digital image]. [Viewed 6 October 2020]. www.facebook.com/shiningmemes/photos/a.756790577864299/1332038090339542

Thibodeau, P., & Boroditsky, L. (2011). Metaphors we think with: The role of metaphor in reasoning. *PLoS ONE* 6(2): e16782.

Ting, V. (2020, April 4). To mask or not to mask: WHO makes U-turn while US, Singapore abandon pandemic advice and tell citizens to start wearing masks. South China Morning Post. Accessed 6 April 2020, www.scmp.com/news/hong-kong/health-environment/article/3078437/mask-or-not-mask-who-makes-u-turn-while-us

Treichler, P. A. (1999) AIDS, homophobia, and biomedical discourse: An epidemic of signification. (1999). In P. A. Treichler (ed.), *How to have theory in an epidemic* (pp. 11–41). Chapel Hill, NC: Duke University Press.

Tufekci, Z. (2020, March 17) Why Telling People They Don't Need Masks Backfired. *The New York Times*. Accessed 20 March 2020, www.nytimes.com/2020/03/17/opinion/coronavirus-face-masks.html

u/rastafaryn (2020). *All of a sudden everybody has become Sheldon* [digital image]. [Viewed 6 October 2020]. www.reddit.com/r/CoronavirusMemes/comments/fi9cp9/all_of_a_sudden_everybody_has_become_sheldon/

United Nations (2019). United Nations strategy and plan of action on hate speech. Accessed 3 May 2020, www.un.org/en/genocideprevention/documents/UN%20Strategy%20and%20Plan%20of%20Action%20on%20Hate%20Speech%2018%20June%20SYNOPSIS.pdf

Van Leeuwen, T., 2007. Legitimation in discourse and communication. *Discourse & communication*, 1(1), pp.91–112.

Vasquez, C., Aslan, E. (2020). 'Cats be outside, how about meow': Multimodal humor and creativity in an internet meme. *Journal of Pragmatics*, 171, 101–117.

Watson, N., Roulstone, A., & Thomas, C. (eds.) (2012). *The Routledge handbook of disability studies*. London: Routledge.

Weale, S. (2020, March 17). Chinese students flee UK after 'maskaphobia' triggered racist attacks. *The Guardian*. Accessed 5 April 2020, www.theguardian.com/education/2020/mar/17/chinese-students-flee-uk-after-maskaphobia-triggered-racist-attacks

Whillock, R. K. 2000. Ethical considerations of civil discourse: The implications of the rise of 'hate speech'. In R. E. Denton, Jr (ed.), *Political communication ethics: An oxymoron?* (pp. 75–90). Westport, CT: Praeger Publishers.

Wodak, R. (2015). Critical discourse analysis, Discourse-historical approach. In K. Tracy, T. Sandel & C. Ilie (eds.), *The International Encyclopedia of Language and Social Interaction*. (pp. 1–14). Chichester: John Wiley & Sons.

Wooller, S., & Mullin, G. (2020, June 19). COVID alert drops to Level 3 paving way for 2m rule relaxation. *The Sun*. Accessed 11 May 2020, www.thesun.co .uk/news/11902656/COVID-alert-level-3-uk/

Wu, L. (1959). *Plague fighter: The autobiography of a modern Chinese physician*. Cambridge: W. Heffer.

Yus, F. (2019). Multimodality in memes: A cyberpragmatic approach. In P. Bou-Franch & P. Garcés-Conejos Blitvich (eds.), *Analyzing digital discourse* (pp. 105–131). Palgrave Macmillan.

Yus, F. (2020). Incongruity-resolution humorous strategies in image macro memes. *Internet Pragmatics*, 1–19.

Zhu, H., Li, W., & Lyons, A. (2017). 'Polish shop(ping) as translanguaging space. *Social Semiotics*, 27 (4), 411–434.

Cambridge Elements ☰

Applied Linguistics

Li Wei
University College London

Li Wei is Chair of Applied Linguistics at the UCL Institute of Education, University College London (UCL), and Fellow of Academy of Social Sciences, UK. His research covers different aspects of bilingualism and multilingualism. He was the founding editor of the following journals: *International Journal of Bilingualism* (Sage), *Applied Linguistics Review* (De Gruyter), *Language, Culture and Society* (Benjamins), *Chinese Language and Discourse* (Benjamins) and *Global Chinese* (De Gruyter), and is currently Editor of the *International Journal of Bilingual Education and Bilingualism* (Taylor and Francis). His books include the *Blackwell Guide to Research Methods in Bilingualism and Multilingualism* (with Melissa Moyer) and *Translanguaging: Language, Bilingualism and Education* (with Ofelia Garcia) which won the British Association of Applied Linguistics Book Prize.

Zhu Hua
University of Birmingham

Zhu Hua is Chair of Educational Linguistics and Director of the MOSAIC Research Group for Multilingualism, School of Education, University of Birmingham. She is Fellow of Academy of Social Sciences, UK. Previously she was Professor of Applied Linguistics in the Department of Applied Linguistics and Communication, Birkbeck College, University of London. Her research is centred around multilingual and intercultural communication. She has also studied child language development and language learning. She is book series co-editor for *Routledge Studies in Language and Intercultural Communication* and *Cambridge Key Topics in Applied Linguistics*, and Forum and Book Reviews Editor of *Applied Linguistics* (Oxford University Press).

About the Series

Mirroring the *Cambridge Key Topics in Applied Linguistics*, this Elements series focuses on the key topics, concepts and methods in Applied Linguistics today. It revisits core conceptual and methodological issues in different subareas of Applied Linguistics. It also explores new emerging themes and topics. All topics are examined in connection with real-world issues and the broader political, economic and ideological contexts.

Cambridge Elements ≡

Applied Linguistics

Elements in the Series

Viral Discourse
Edited by Rodney H. Jones

A full series listing is available at www.cambridge.org/EIAL

Printed in the United States
by Baker & Taylor Publisher Services

Printed in the United States
by Baker & Taylor Publisher Services